50% OFF
Online NCMHCE Prep Course!

by Mometrix

Dear Customer,

We consider it an honor and a privilege that you chose to study for the NCMHCE with us. As a way of showing our appreciation and to help us better serve you, we are offering **50% off our online NCMHCE Prep Course**. Many NCMHCE courses are needlessly expensive and don't deliver enough value. With our course, you get access to the best NCMHCE prep material, and **you only pay half price**.

We have structured our online course to perfectly complement your printed test prep. The NCMHCE Prep Course contains **in-depth lessons** that cover all the most important topics, **video reviews** that explain difficult concepts, **practice questions** to ensure you feel prepared, and more than **450 digital flashcards**, so you can study while you're on the go.

Online NCMHCE Prep Course

Topics Included:

- Professional Practice and Ethics
- Intake, Assessment, and Diagnosis
- Areas of Clinical Focus
- Treatment Planning
- Counseling Skills and Interventions
- Core Counseling Attributes

Course Features:

- NCMHCE Study Guide
  - Get content that complements our best-selling study guide.
- Full-Length Practice Tests
  - With hundreds of practice questions, you can test yourself again and again.
- Mobile Friendly
  - If you need to study on the go, the course is easily accessible from your mobile device.
- NCMHCE Flashcards
  - Our course includes a flashcard mode with more than 450 content cards to help you study.

To receive this discount, visit us at mometrix.com/university/ncmhce or simply scan this QR code with your smartphone. At the checkout page, enter the discount code: **ncmhce50off**

If you have any questions or concerns, please contact us at support@mometrix.com.

TEST PREPARATION

FREE Study Skills Videos/DVD Offer

Dear Customer,

Thank you for your purchase from Mometrix! We consider it an honor and a privilege that you have purchased our product and we want to ensure your satisfaction.

As part of our ongoing effort to meet the needs of test takers, we have developed a set of Study Skills Videos that we would like to give you for <u>FREE</u>. These videos cover our *best practices* for getting ready for your exam, from how to use our study materials to how to best prepare for the day of the test.

All that we ask is that you email us with feedback that would describe your experience so far with our product. Good, bad, or indifferent, we want to know what you think!

To get your FREE Study Skills Videos, you can use the **QR code** below, or send us an **email** at <u>studyvideos@mometrix.com</u> with *FREE VIDEOS* in the subject line and the following information in the body of the email:

- The name of the product you purchased.
- Your product rating on a scale of 1-5, with 5 being the highest rating.
- Your feedback. It can be long, short, or anything in between. We just want to know your impressions and experience so far with our product. (Good feedback might include how our study material met your needs and ways we might be able to make it even better. You could highlight features that you found helpful or features that you think we should add.)

If you have any questions or concerns, please don't hesitate to contact me directly.

Thanks again!

Sincerely,

Jay Willis
Vice President
<u>jay.willis@mometrix.com</u>
1-800-673-8175

NCMHCE
Exam
Practice Questions

NCMHCE Practice Test Review for the
National Clinical Mental Health
Counseling Examination

Written and edited by the Mometrix Counselor Certification Test Team

Printed in the United States of America

This paper meets the requirements of ANSI/NISO Z39.48-1992 (Permanence of Paper).

Mometrix offers volume discount pricing to institutions. For more information or a price quote, please contact our sales department at sales@mometrix.com or 888-248-1219.

ISBN 13: 978-1-5167-2071-2
ISBN 10: 1-5167-2071-7

DEAR FUTURE EXAM SUCCESS STORY

First of all, **THANK YOU** for purchasing Mometrix study materials!

Second, congratulations! You are one of the few determined test-takers who are committed to doing whatever it takes to excel on your exam. **You have come to the right place.** We developed these practice tests with one goal in mind: to deliver you the best possible approximation of the questions you will see on test day.

Standardized testing is one of the biggest obstacles on your road to success, which only increases the importance of doing well in the high-pressure, high-stakes environment of test day. Your results on this test could have a significant impact on your future, and these practice tests will give you the repetitions you need to build your familiarity and confidence with the test content and format to help you achieve your full potential on test day.

Your success is our success

We would love to hear from you! If you would like to share the story of your exam success or if you have any questions or comments in regard to our products, please contact us at **800-673-8175** or **support@mometrix.com**.

Thanks again for your business and we wish you continued success!

Sincerely,
The Mometrix Test Preparation Team

TABLE OF CONTENTS

NCMHCE Practice Test #1

Case Study 1

PART ONE

INTAKE

CLIENT

Age: 42

Sex: Female

Gender: Female

Sexuality: Heterosexual

Ethnicity: Caucasian

Relationship Status: Divorced

Counseling Setting: Agency

Type of Counseling: Individual and Group

Presenting Problem: Social Anxiety

Diagnosis: Social Anxiety Disorder (Social Phobia), Provisional 300.23 (F 40.10)

PRESENTING PROBLEM:

You are a certified mental health counselor working in a community mental health center. Your client is a 42-year-old white female who presents today with symptoms of social anxiety disorder. The client reports debilitating anxiety when interacting with others, particularly when meeting unfamiliar people or going somewhere for the first time. She states that she cannot sleep and has a poor appetite on the days leading up to social events. When encountering anxiety-provoking situations, she says that her hands shake, she sweats excessively, and her voice trembles. The client is recently divorced and, after more than 15 years of being out of the workforce, she is seeking employment. She explains that job interviews have been "humiliating" because of what she perceives as an "inherent lack of knowledge and a substantially impaired skill set."

MENTAL STATUS:

The client is meticulously dressed and well groomed. She is cooperative and periodically exhibits a nervous smile. The client is fidgety and frequently repositions herself when seated. Her mood is anxious, and she becomes tearful when discussing feeling "stupid" during job interviews. She exhibits cohesive thinking, and her insight and judgment are intact. The client is oriented to person, place, situation, and time. Her affect is reserved. She denies suicidal and homicidal ideation as well as audio/visual hallucinations.

HISTORY OF CONDITION:

The client first noticed symptoms of social anxiety when her family moved north during the summer of her 8th-grade school year. When she began high school, she received unwanted attention for being the "new girl." She explains that she was often teased because of her Southern

1

accent and was labeled "country" and "ignorant." Before meeting her husband, the client remembers drinking before going on a date stating, "It just helped settle my nerves." Her social anxiety lessened after becoming a stay-at-home mom to her two now-teenage children. However, she noticed a sharp increase in social anxiety after her divorce, particularly when attempting to reenter the job force and trying to find new social circles. She denies current drug use and states that she is a social drinker.

FAMILY HISTORY:

The client's parents both live out of town and run a business together. The client's father has been treated for alcohol use disorder and is now in recovery. Her mother takes medication for anxiety and depression. The client has two teenage girls. Both girls have had a difficult time with the divorce. Her youngest child is seeing a therapist for depression. The client's ex-husband is a prominent attorney in their town. This is the client's first experience with counseling, and she asks many questions when filling out the intake paperwork.

1. To accurately diagnose social anxiety disorder, individuals must experience marked fear or anxiety in social situations and which of the following?
   a. Fear of being incapacitated by an unforeseen panic attack in public
   b. Fear of social situations because of perceived appearance-related flaws
   c. Fear of acting in ways that other people will scrutinize
   d. Fear of not being able to escape certain situations in the presence of profound anxiety

2. You cover administrative and clinical protocols when reviewing paperwork with the client, including the Health Insurance Portability and Accountability Act of 1996 (HIPAA) Privacy Rule. Which one of the following statements is true of HIPAA?
   a. HIPAA ensures that confidential information will not be used in legal proceedings.
   b. HIPAA serves as an authorization (i.e., consent) to counseling services.
   c. HIPAA gives clients the right to be informed of privacy and confidentiality policies before providing consent.
   d. HIPAA protects and safeguards confidential electronic records from potential security risks.

3. You help the client create self-affirmations to counter the anxiety that she experiences during job interviews. According to self-affirmation theory, what is the first step to developing these mental processes?
   a. Identify the activating event.
   b. Identify a significant core value.
   c. Model unconditional positive regard.
   d. Replace a crossed transaction with a complementary transaction.

4. You and another counselor would like to start a group for individuals with social anxiety who tend to avoid performance situations (e.g., talking in front of others, taking an exam, interviews, etc.). Which instrument would you use to help measure this?
   a. Hamilton Anxiety Rating Scale
   b. Liebowitz Social Anxiety Scale
   c. Beck Anxiety Inventory
   d. Fear Questionnaire Social Phobia Subscale

5. The client is resistant to engage in the self-affirmation exercise, exclaiming that "It just seems silly." Using motivational interviewing, which response would best increase her compliance with this activity?

    a. "Change is really hard for you, but I think you'll be pleased with the results."
    b. "There are now studies showing that positive affirmations activate neural reward pathways in the brain."
    c. "You feel like I don't understand you or can't help you."
    d. "This way of decreasing anxiety seems foreign to you."

6. The client has agreed to participate in a cognitive behavioral therapy (CBT) group for social anxiety. You co-lead the group and would like the members to experience universality, one of Irvin Yalom's curative factors. Which technique would best enable you to do so?

    a. Facilitating
    b. Interpreting
    c. Linking
    d. Confronting

PART TWO

FIRST SESSION, 6 WEEKS AFTER THE INITIAL INTAKE

The client attends a process-oriented CBT group that is nearing the middle stage of group development. The client presents today with a bright affect and arrives early to converse with two other women in the group. During group activities, she is reticent to share and is sensitive to a conflict between two members that has started to emerge. One member becomes openly critical of the group tasks and their usefulness. Other members start to weigh in and take sides. The conflict quickly escalates between two members, with one shouting at another, "You have monopolized every session with your opinions. You are the most judgmental person I know! This group would be so much better without you." Other members nod in agreement.

7. How would a gestalt therapist describe the boundary disturbance that characterizes the group member's statements of "You have monopolized every session with your opinions. You are the most judgmental person I know! This group would be so much better without you"?

    a. Introjection
    b. Deflection
    c. Confluence
    d. Projection

8. As the leader of this process-oriented group, what is your best response to the emerging conflict?

    a. "I'd like to pause for a moment and remind everyone of the group rules."
    b. "What core beliefs might underlie the strong opinions expressed today?"
    c. "How might removing a member deprive you of learning from one another?"
    d. "Let's explore ways that we have all responded to difficult people in our lives."

9. After processing the conflict, what technique could you use to help group members recognize significant themes and patterns?

   a. Genuineness
   b. Unconditional positive regard
   c. Empathetic reflection
   d. Summarization

PART THREE
SECOND SESSION, 12 WEEKS AFTER THE INITIAL INTAKE

The client participates in her last group therapy session today. You and the client review her treatment plan goals, and she reports an overall decrease in anxiety and says that she possesses a greater awareness of social anxiety disorder and the associated interventions. She has recently completed a job interview after previously scheduling and canceling two interviews. She plans to stay in touch with two group members. The client is ready to begin termination but is anxious about ending counseling. You and the client review the psychoeducation material reviewed in the group, including factors associated with social anxiety disorder and learned coping strategies.

10. Which of the following is true of factors related to social anxiety?

   a. Relaxation and other safety behaviors are helpful for managing social anxiety.
   b. Individuals with social anxiety underestimate how negatively others judge them.
   c. In feared social situations, avoidance behaviors help maintain anxiety.
   d. Postevent rumination helps accurately evaluate feared outcomes.

11. The client recognizes gains that she has made but fears that she will fail after discharge. Which humanistic technique would you use to best respond to this discrepancy?

   a. Constructive confrontation
   b. Amplified reflection
   c. Attending
   d. Self-disclosure

12. You would like to measure the effectiveness of the group intervention by administering the same standardized instrument that was used previously to measure social performance and anxiety This experimental design is an example of which of the following?

   a. One-group pretest-posttest
   b. One-group posttest comparison
   c. One-shot case study
   d. Two-group nonrandom-selection pretest-posttest

13. You previously measured the effectiveness of the group intervention by administering the same standardized instrument that was once used to measure social performance anxiety. Which one of the following serves as your independent variable?

   a. The group intervention
   b. Social performance anxiety
   c. The instrument used in the pretest
   d. The instrument used in the posttest

Case Study 2

PART ONE
INTAKE
CLIENT

Age: 26

Sex: Male

Gender: Male

Sexuality: Heterosexual

Ethnicity: African American

Relationship Status: Single

Counseling Setting: Community Mental Health Center

Type of Counseling: Individual

Presenting Problem: Depressive Symptoms

Diagnosis: Persistent Depressive Disorder (PDD) (Dysthymia) Diagnostic Criteria 300.4 (F34.1)

PRESENTING PROBLEM:

You are a counselor working in a community mental health center. Your initial intake appointment is with a 26-year-old African American male who presents with symptoms of depression. The client states that he has felt depressed since his teens, with symptoms increasing within the last couple of months. He reports feelings of worthlessness, fatigue, and occasional bouts of insomnia. In addition, the client indicates that his symptoms worsened after his girlfriend of 2 years broke things off with him. He explained that she grew tired of his low energy and pessimistic outlook on life. As a result, he has been hesitant to seek help, believing that he just needed to "man up" and handle his problems privately. The client is unsure of his insurance benefits but thinks his policy allows for a limited number of counseling sessions.

MENTAL STATUS EXAM:

The client is dressed in age-appropriate clothing and is well groomed. His affect is blunted and anxious at times. The client denies anxiety but discloses that he is nervous about the counseling process and doesn't know what to expect. He is cooperative but hesitant to offer more information than is asked. The client is tearful when discussing his breakup and states that there are days when it is a struggle to get out of bed and go to work. He denies suicidal ideation, and he says that he has had no previous attempts. The client is oriented to person, place, time, and situation, and his thought content is organized.

FAMILY AND WORK HISTORY:

The client grew up in a home with his mother, father, and maternal grandmother. He has a 22-year-old sister who he believes also experiences depression, but he is unsure if she has received treatment. The client says that he attends church "most Sundays" with his family, primarily because he knows it is important to his grandmother. The client holds an associate degree in information technology and is a computer network support specialist. He has worked for the same company for the past 4 years.

1. The client is unsure of his insurance benefits and allotted counseling sessions. You review his benefits plan and any associated fees as part of which of the following?

    a. The confidentiality agreement
    b. The client's privacy rights
    c. An explanation of limitations
    d. The process of informed consent

2. Considering the client's hesitancy to participate in counseling, which of the following instruments would you select to better understand his help-seeking behaviors?

    a. Ethnic-Sensitive Inventory (ESI)
    b. Cultural Formulation Interview (CFI)
    c. Munroe Multicultural Attitude Scale Questionnaire (MASQUE)
    d. Iowa Cultural Understanding Assessment—Client Form

3. You would like to use the Beck Depression Inventory-II (BDI-II) but are concerned about the possibility of racial bias. You find a study stating, "The recommended cutoff score of 14 for screening for depression appears to be appropriate for African-American patients in the primary care setting" (Dutton et al., 2004). This cutoff yielded a specificity of 84%. How do you interpret these findings?

    a. 84% of respondents without depression scored below 14.
    b. 84% of respondents with depression scored above 14.
    c. 84% of respondents have a high probability of scoring above 14.
    d. 84% of respondents have a low probability of scoring above 14.

4. A separate study found that the BDI-II was significantly correlated with the Patient Health Questionnaire (PHQ-9), which is evidence of which one of the following?

    a. Predictive validity
    b. Criterion-related validity
    c. Convergent validity
    d. Test-retest reliability

5. Which is true of the American Psychological Association (APA)'s Diagnostic and Statistical Manual of Mental Disorders (DSM-5) inclusion criteria for persistent depressive disorder (PDD) and major depressive disorder (MDD)?

    a. PDD includes possible experiences of anhedonia; MDD does not.
    b. PDD includes recurrent suicidality without a plan; MDD includes suicidality with a plan.
    c. PDD symptoms must persist for more days than not for at least 1 year; MDD symptoms must persist every day for at least 2 weeks.
    d. PDD includes feelings of hopelessness; MDD includes feelings of worthlessness or inappropriate guilt.

6. Which approach would you implement to help understand the influence of the client's social and cultural factors, including systemic racism, gender, religion, and birth order?

    a. Adlerian
    b. Freudian
    c. Gestalt
    d. Rogerian

PART TWO

FIRST SESSION, 4 WEEKS AFTER THE INITIAL INTAKE

You learn that the client withheld information during the intake interview because of a negative experience with psychiatric treatment. Two years previously, the client presented at the emergency room with symptoms of depression and suicidal ideation. The emergency department clinician recommended hospitalization, and the client complied. During his hospital stay, he was placed on an antipsychotic medication for paranoia and was diagnosed with schizoaffective disorder. Although the client admits to suicidal ideation, he denies ever experiencing paranoia. He reports having side effects from the medication and immediately discontinued it after discharge. The client states that he has been very depressed since the breakup with his girlfriend and was willing to give counseling another try before his depression "hit rock bottom."

7. After disclosing his experience with hospitalization, the client asks questions about your credentials, counseling approach, and experience. What would be your first response?

    a. Shift the focus back to the client and emphasize the importance of honest communication regarding suicidality.
    b. Provide a written copy of informed consent, which includes your credentials and related information.
    c. Understand and validate the client's experience with hospitalization and consider contextualized factors.
    d. Obtain a signed release of information to communicate with the hospital and request the client's records.

8. Which approach emphasizes establishing a therapeutic alliance upon which you can safely examine the client's cognitive distortions?

    a. Rational-emotive behavior therapy
    b. Cognitive therapy
    c. Psychoanalytic therapy
    d. Person-centered therapy

9. Which of the following would you select to evaluate the client's cognitive distortions by testing them against sound logic and reason?

    a. Counterconditioning
    b. Socratic questioning
    c. Forceful disputing
    d. Assuming responsibility

PART THREE

SECOND SESSION, 8 WEEKS AFTER THE INITIAL INTAKE

The client has responded well to identifying automatic thoughts and distorted thinking. Although some depressive symptoms have decreased, he reports continued distress stemming from the breakup with his girlfriend. He believes that he is "unworthy of love" and is destined to fail in his intimate relationships. Despite his progress in identifying cognitive distortions, the client reports feeling stuck. You and the client discuss your theoretical orientation, the therapeutic relationship, and the treatment plan goals and objectives. The client says that he values your collaborative approach, believes that the two of you have a strong working relationship, and agrees with the

overall therapy goals. Despite slight improvement with his depressive symptoms, he is committed to therapy and trusts the process.

10. You gather information to identify factors impeding the client's progress. How would you incorporate the influence of emotional, cognitive, and behavioral factors on the client's clinical presentation and plan of care?

    a. Construct a case conceptualization.
    b. Summarize the client's reasons for feeling stuck.
    c. Obtain an interdisciplinary consultation.
    d. Conduct a functional behavioral analysis.

11. The client believes he is unworthy of love and destined to fail in intimate relationships. This is an example of which one of the following?

    a. Personalization
    b. Overgeneralization
    c. Black-and-white thinking
    d. Confirmation bias

12. To facilitate the client's progress, which of the following would you use to help access the client's underlying core beliefs about himself, others, and the world?

    a. The downward arrow technique
    b. The memory rescripting technique
    c. The hidden emotion technique
    d. The scaling technique

13. Once a core belief is identified, which cognitive restructuring technique would you select to help reduce psychological distress?

    a. Shame-attacking exercises
    b. Identify the "three basic musts"
    c. Role reversion
    d. Ask exception questions

Case Study 3

PART ONE
INTAKE
CLIENT

Age: 13

Sex Assigned at Birth: Male

Gender: Transgender; Gender Nonconforming (TGNC)

Ethnicity: Caucasian

Counseling Setting: Child and Family Agency, School-Based Services

Type of Counseling: Individual and Family

Presenting Problem: Truancy; Gender Dysphoria

Diagnosis: Gender Dysphoria, Provisional (F64.1); Social Exclusion or Rejection V62.4 (Z60.4)

PRESENTING PROBLEM:

You are a school-based mental health counselor in a public middle school. Your client is a 13-year-old Caucasian 7th grader who presents for the initial intake with their mother. The mother says that the client has had several unexcused absences from school because "he is confused about his gender." The client adamantly denies being confused and explains that they self-identify as transgender. The client's preferred pronouns are "they/them." The client further states that they have had a strong desire to be a different gender since early childhood, and this desire and their distress have recently intensified. The mother reports that the client is chronically irritable, spends a lot of time alone, and has "basically shut everyone out." The client reports experiencing bullying—both verbal and physical—in school "nearly every day." In addition to the bullying, the client says that certain teachers refuse to allow them to use the bathroom aligned with their identified gender. To prevent this conflict, the client does not eat breakfast or lunch at school.

MENTAL STATUS EXAM:

The client is dressed in age-appropriate clothing. They wear eye makeup and chipped black fingernail polish, and they have bitten most fingernails down to the quick. The client's mood is irritable, and they are quick to show anger toward their mother when misgendered. Their thoughts are coherent, and they deny audio/visual hallucinations. The client acknowledges feeling sad and hopeless but denies suicidal ideation. They attribute increased levels of anxiety at school to bullying, particularly with select peers. They explain that a select group of students threaten the client and call them offensive and derogatory names.

FAMILY HISTORY AND HISTORY OF THE PRESENTING PROBLEM:

The client's mother and father are both realtors. The mother states that she used to see a therapist for anxiety, which she now manages with medication. The father works long hours, and the mother returns home early to attend to the client's needs. The mother states that she realized that the client wished to be another gender when they were younger, but she believed it was just a phase. She explains that the father is not supportive and refuses to discuss the issue. The mother is concerned about the client's truancy and desires to be supportive but has mixed feelings about it. She says that she is fearful every day and believes that if she accepts the client's truth, it will set the child up for "a lifetime of prejudice and discrimination."

1. Which one of the following is an accurate depiction of gender identity?
   a. One's conception of being either male, female, or something else
   b. One's outward expression as being either male, female, or something else
   c. Congruence between one's gender identity, gender expression, and gender assigned at birth
   d. Incongruence between one's experienced/expressed gender and gender assigned at birth

2. The DSM-5 defines gender dysphoria as distress stemming from a marked incongruence between one's assigned gender and which of the following?
   a. One's preferred gender
   b. One's reassigned gender
   c. One's experienced gender
   d. One's suppressed gender

3. Preventing the client from using a gender-neutral restroom or a restroom that corresponds to their gender identity violates which one of the following?
   a. The Family Educational Rights and Privacy Act of 1974 (FERPA)
   b. Title IX of the Education Amendments of 1972
   c. The First Amendment of the United States Constitution
   d. Title II of the Americans with Disabilities Act (ADA)

4. Bullying is defined as behaviors that include all of the following components EXCEPT:
   a. Actions that are intentionally aggressive or mean
   b. Behaviors that are repeated over time
   c. Situations involving an imbalance of power
   d. Behaviors within a larger school or community setting

5. Your religious beliefs prohibit you from affirming the gender identity of a 13-year-old. Which of the following is your best first response?
   a. Self-disclose your misgivings with the mother to help establish a therapeutic alliance.
   b. Conduct a trauma-informed assessment to determine the etiology of the client's gender identity to help refine the treatment focus.
   c. Use self-reflection and self-assessment to examine the personal biases and stereotypes you may have about transgender individuals.
   d. Refer the client to a counselor who specializes in counseling transgender youths to prevent imposing your personally held values and beliefs.

6. Which of the following suggests that gender dysphoria is caused not only by external (distal) stressors (e.g., prejudice, discrimination) but also by internalized (proximal) stressors (transphobia, stigma)?
   a. Cognitive dissonance theory
   b. Minority stress theory
   c. Social identity theory
   d. Escape theory

PART TWO

FIRST SESSION, 4 WEEKS AFTER THE INITIAL INTAKE

Since the intake, you have provided professional development training for school staff on transgender and gender nonconforming (TGNC) individuals. The administration supports your recommendations for keeping the client and others safe at school. The client continues to miss school, but they have had fewer absences this month. You learn that the client's desire to be rid of their male secondary sex characteristics has become more persistent. They say that they have seen media coverage of individuals who have undergone sex reassignment surgeries and wondered what that would be like. The client also states they are confused about their sexual orientation. The client appreciates being an active participant in their treatment, and together you create relevant treatment plan goals. You discuss the upcoming family session with the client's parents. The client articulates appropriate topics for this session and reports increased anxiety concerning their father's participation.

7. Based on the client's diagnosis, which treatment plan goal would you select for the client?
   a. To reduce distress caused by the desire to identify as another gender
   b. To reduce incongruence between gender expression and gender identity
   c. To reduce distress caused by sexual orientation uncertainty
   d. To reduce incongruence between nonbinary and cisgender identity

8. What is the primary purpose for inviting the client to be an active participant in their treatment?
   a. To present as a united front during the upcoming family session
   b. To validate presenting concerns and establish hope
   c. To model active listening and express empathy
   d. To help the client gain confidence in self-advocacy

9. Counselors must carefully examine the benefits and risks associated with medical interventions for adolescents with gender dysphoria. Which ethical principle considers the client's capacity to participate in the decision-making process?
   a. Beneficence
   b. Justice
   c. Fidelity
   d. Autonomy

PART THREE

SECOND SESSION, 6 WEEKS AFTER THE INITIAL INTAKE

You work with the client and their parents to help the parents understand how the client conceptualizes their gender identity. You use the client's self-identified, gender-affirming pronouns and praise the client for taking a brave first step. The client's mother is fearful and anxious, particularly when thinking about the client's safety. The client's father expresses an overall lack of understanding and thinks it could be a phase. You recognize the father's efforts to understand and help the client explain the distressing emotions associated with coming to terms with their gender identity, including an increase in severity since the onset of adolescence. The father states that he is unsure if he can accept the client's transgender identity but says that he is committed to the counseling process.

10. What is the main purpose of supporting the client's use of self-identified, gender-affirming pronouns?
    a. To lay the groundwork for reparative therapy as an evidence-based practice (EBP)
    b. To illustrate potential difficulties associated with social transitions
    c. To help the parents become acclimated to the lifelong use of the client's selected pronouns
    d. To normalize and validate gender diversity as a natural human variation

11. Your goal is to deliberately disrupt the family's homeostasis through unbalancing, blocking transactional patterns, and shifting boundaries. These techniques are associated with which one of the following?
    a. Contextual family therapy
    b. Structural family therapy
    c. Multigenerational family therapy
    d. Strategic family therapy

12. The client is discouraged by their father's lack of acceptance. Which of the following can you use to reconceptualize the client's perception by shifting their viewpoint?
    a. Restructuring
    b. Linking
    c. Reframing
    d. Joining

13. You provide ongoing assessment for any associated mental disorders that may further complicate the client's coming out process. According to the DSM-5, gender dysphoria is comorbid with all of the following EXCEPT:
    a. Anxiety disorders
    b. Depressive disorders
    c. Autism spectrum disorder
    d. Attention-deficit/hyperactivity disorder (ADHD)

Case Study 4

PART ONE

INTAKE

CLIENT

Age/Gender:

- Wife: 34-Year-Old Female
- Husband: 44-Year-Old Male

Sexuality: Both Heterosexual

Ethnicity: Both Caucasian

Relationship Status: Married

Counseling Setting: Outpatient Behavioral Health

Type of Counseling: Couples Counseling

Presenting Problem: Marital Discord

Diagnoses:

- Wife: Depressive Disorder Due to Another Medical Condition (Migraine Headache), Provisional (F06.31)
- Husband: Alcohol Use Disorder, in Sustained Remission, Provisional (F10.20)

PRESENTING PROBLEM:

You are a certified counselor providing couples therapy in an outpatient behavioral health setting. The wife serves as the primary client due to the complexity of her clinical and diagnostic presentation. She is a 34-year-old female seeking marital counseling with her 44-year-old husband of 18 months. The client explains that shortly after returning from the couple's honeymoon, she began having chronic, debilitating migraines causing her to remain bedridden, sometimes for days on end. She reports that she no longer engages in activities that she once enjoyed and feels chronically tired and depressed. Despite being treated by several neurologists, her chronic migraines persist, and she is now on long-term leave from her job. The client's husband is a chief financial officer for a large hospital system and works long hours. The couple has joint custody of the husband's 12-year-old son from a previous marriage. The client thinks that there is an unfair amount of burden placed on her to parent her stepchild, which has caused conflict among the client, her husband, and the husband's ex-wife. The husband admits to growing impatient with the chronic nature of his wife's illness and says she is not the same person that she was when they met nearly 3 years ago.

MENTAL STATUS EXAM:

The client and the husband are both well dressed. The client is wearing sunglasses and explains that her migraines cause her to be light sensitive. It is the middle of the husband's workday, and he is dressed in a suit and tie. The client reports daytime sleepiness, which she attributes to her migraine medication. Her appetite is fair. She denies current suicidal or homicidal ideations. However, the client does report that she has previously had thoughts of not wanting to live. Her mood is depressed, and her affect is congruent with her mood. The client is tearful when discussing how her illness has affected the marriage and states that she receives little support from her husband. When the client begins to cry, the husband responds by sitting silently, crossing his arms, shaking his head, and looking around the room. The client states, "See! This is what I'm talking about! Whenever I need his support, he checks out."

<u>FAMILY HISTORY AND HISTORY OF PRESENTING PROBLEM:</u>

The client's parents were never married. The client was placed in foster care at age 3 due to parental neglect. She remained in foster care until age 6, when the courts granted her paternal grandmother full custody. The client's husband has two younger brothers and was raised by his biological mother and father. He describes his father as "hardworking" and his mother as a stay-at-home mom. Approximately 5 years ago, the husband was treated for alcohol use disorder. He states that he stopped drinking independently and "didn't have to rely on a 12-step program to get sober." The couple met when the husband was married, which contributed to a drawn-out and acrimonious divorce.

1. The diagnosis of depressive disorder due to another medical condition (migraine headache) can be assigned when the disturbance is caused by which of the following?

    a.   The physiological effects of migraine medication
    b.   The pathophysiological effects of migraine headache
    c.   The biopsychosocial effects of migraine headache and/or migraine medication
    d.   The psychocultural effects of migraine headache

2. Research indicates that depression and migraine headaches may be reduced by engaging in an activity involving tensing and releasing muscle groups. This is an example of which one of the following?

    a.   Biofeedback training
    b.   Progressive relaxation
    c.   Autogenic training
    d.   Rhythmic breathing

3. What assessment tool should you use to better determine the couple's relationship distress, cohesiveness, and affectional expression?

    a.   Dyadic Adjustment Scale (DAS)
    b.   Maudsley Marital Questionnaire (MMQ)
    c.   Personal Assessment of Intimacy in Relationships (PAIR)
    d.   Measure of Attachment Qualities (MAQ)

4. During the initial session, which of the following would you use to create a therapeutic alliance with the couple?

    a.   Explain your clinical approach to help define the treatment focus.
    b.   Empathize with and validate the client's physical and emotional pain.
    c.   Summarize the couple's concerns and assess readiness for change.
    d.   Encourage the use of "I" statements and teach effective problem solving.

5. Which one of the following methods treats childhood trauma by using bilateral stimulation to activate portions of the brain and release blocked emotional experiences?

    a.   Neuro-linguistic programming
    b.   Acceptance and commitment therapy
    c.   Eye movement desensitization and reprocessing
    d.   Interpersonal psychotherapy

6. Which approach considers the implications of the client's early childhood experiences in the context of the couple's clinical presentation?

    a. Person-centered couples therapy
    b. Cognitive-behavioral couples therapy
    c. Emotionally focused couples therapy
    d. Solution-focused relationship therapy

PART TWO

FIRST SESSION, 4 WEEKS AFTER THE INITIAL INTAKE

The couple acknowledge some improvement with communication, but they continue to feel significant levels of relationship distress. The client has been asking for what she needs, mainly when she is in pain and functionally limited, but she reports that the husband continues to do little to support her. The husband reiterates that he has a demanding job that depletes his energy and that he has little to give when he gets home at night. The husband's child has been verbally abusive to the client, and her husband minimizes her concern. The client feels "stuck in the middle" when determining her stepson's schedule and activities. The client states that her husband's bitter ex-wife makes her new role as stepparent "nearly impossible." To help with the postdivorce adjustment and lessen conflict, you provide information on local support groups, parent education programs through family court, and additional educational resources.

7. You provide educational resources outlining your parenting recommendations. Which of the following would most benefit all involved parties?

    a. Cooperative parenting
    b. Parallel parenting
    c. Collaborative parenting
    d. Authoritative parenting

8. The client expresses negative beliefs about herself, her world, and her future. Which one of the following theorists described this as the cognitive triad?

    a. Albert Ellis
    b. William Glasser
    c. Aaron Beck
    d. Frederick Perls

9. The client states, "His ex-wife makes coparenting nearly impossible, and he continues to do absolutely nothing about it!" You state, "Can you turn to him and tell him what that is like for you?" What are you trying to accomplish with your request?

    a. Create new experiences of emotional attachment.
    b. Increase change talk by reducing ambivalence.
    c. Assess for transference and countertransference.
    d. Help him "mirror" back the emotional content.

10. The imago intentional dialogue technique with couples consists of three steps. In step 2, you encourage the message receiver to respond by stating, "You make sense because ..." or "I can see where ..." This is an example of which of the following?

    a. Attending
    b. Empathizing
    c. Summarizing
    d. Validating

PART THREE
SECOND SESSION, 8 WEEKS AFTER THE INITIAL INTAKE

The client arrives for the session without her husband. Her affect is flat, and she presents as more subdued. The client explains that she has been in bed for the last 4 days, which has caused escalated conflict and tension with her husband. She says that her husband believes that they are at an impasse and threatened to leave during their fight last night. When processing the details of their altercation, the client states that her fear of being alone has become unbearable. She denies any suicidal plans but says she feels hopeless and void of purpose and is in significant levels of physical pain due to intractable migraines. You conduct a suicide risk assessment to determine the client's level of safety.

11. Which instrument would you select to provide a comprehensive suicide risk assessment with the client?
- a. Patient Health Questionnaire-2
- b. Achenbach System of Empirically Based Assessment
- c. Columbia-Suicide Severity Rating Scale
- d. Ask Suicide-Screening Questions Toolkit

12. You ask the client "What are your reasons for living?" What are you are trying to determine with this question?
- a. The level of marital distress
- b. Protective factors
- c. Religious or spiritual support
- d. The appropriate level of care

13. The National Action Alliance for Suicide Prevention (2018) evidence-based standard care for people with suicide risk includes all of the following elements EXCEPT:
- a. Safety planning
- b. Means reduction
- c. Supervision
- d. Caring contacts

Case Study 5

PART ONE

INTAKE

CLIENT

Age: 15

Sex: Female

Gender: Female

Sexual Orientation: Heterosexual

Ethnicity: African American

Counseling Setting: Agency

Type of Counseling: Individual and Group

Presenting Problem: Anxiety

Diagnosis: Generalized Anxiety Disorder (GAD) 300.02 (F41.1)

PRESENTING PROBLEM:

You are a counselor working in a child and family outpatient mental health center. Your client is a 15-year-old African American female enrolled in the 10th grade at a predominately white private high school. She presents today with her father, who says she "has not been herself lately." The client reports that she is under an enormous amount of pressure to excel academically and athletically. She is the number-one ranked player on the varsity tennis team and is in the school's honors program. The client states that she perseverates the night before a tennis match and worries that her performance will be subpar. She reports excessively practicing her serves and backhands in her spare time because she is constantly dissatisfied with her less-than-perfect performance. The client says that she feels like she doesn't fit in with her peers, which she attributes to being the only person of color on her tennis team, and one of few in the student body.

MENTAL STATUS EXAM:

The client is dressed in age-appropriate clothing and is neat in appearance. She is cooperative and, at times, overly compliant with the interview questions, which is exemplified by apologizing unnecessarily for "not answering questions in the right way." Her eye contact is poor, but she is engaged in the interview process. The client is restless and fidgety, and her tone of voice is soft. She states that she gets between 5 and 6 hours of sleep each night, which makes her irritable at times. Her affect is anxious, and she reports poor concentration. Her excessive worry has resulted in exhaustion and feeling like she is "always playing catch-up" with sleep and schoolwork. She denies any suicidal or homicidal ideations. The client also denies drug or alcohol use.

FAMILY HISTORY AND HISTORY OF THE PRESENTING PROBLEM:

The client's milestones for walking, talking, and toilet training were all developmentally appropriate. The client is the only child of parents who divorced when the client was 5 years old. She states that she has always been a worrier and remembers seeing the school counselor in kindergarten for separation anxiety. Her father has physical custody of the client, and her mother sees the client at regular visitation intervals. The father is a tennis pro, and her mother works as a fitness trainer. The client describes her parents as "type A" and explains, "They are always pushing me to my limit." The client's mother has panic attacks, which the client believes are manageable with medication. Her maternal grandmother was an alcoholic who died when her mother was younger. There are no reported mental health issues on the paternal side of the family.

1. The client reports being treated for separation anxiety disorder in kindergarten. You think that the diagnosis is likely based on which of the following DSM-5 criteria?

a. Persistent and excessive fear of teachers and peers
b. Hypervigilance, poor concentration, and sleep disturbance
c. Selective mutism when anticipating being away from home
d. Repeated nightmares involving being away from home

2. Which cardinal feature differentiates generalized anxiety disorder (GAD) from other anxiety-related disorders?

a. The presence of an acute stressor
b. Separation from attachment figures
c. Intrusive thoughts or images
d. Chronic apprehensive expectation

3. For adolescents, hypothesized psychological vulnerabilities for GAD include which of the following?

a. Sleep irregularity
b. Autonomic hyperreactivity
c. Positive valence systems
d. Cognitive biases

4. The client shares her worries about her less-than-perfect performance on the tennis court. This is an example of which of the following?

a. Mind reading
b. Disqualifying the positive
c. Emotional reasoning
d. Black-and-white thinking

5. During the initial stages of therapy, which of the following would best enhance the family's motivation and adherence to treatment?

a. Offering a selection from a variety of treatment modalities (e.g., individual, group, family)
b. Integrating contextualized factors (e.g., cultural, spiritual) into treatment interventions
c. Coordinating treatment with youth-serving systems (e.g., educational, medical)
d. Providing written information explaining the components of informed consent

6. Which one of the following anxiety rating scales includes a version that allows a parent to fill out scales on their child?

a. The Generalized Anxiety Disorder-7 (GAD-7)
b. The abbreviated Conners Parent Rating Scale (CPRS-HI)
c. Hamilton Anxiety Rating Scale (HAM-A)
d. Patient Health Questionnaire (PHQ-9): Parent Report

PART TWO

FIRST SESSION, 6 WEEKS AFTER THE INITIAL INTAKE

The client is responding well to your therapeutic interventions. School has ended, and her summertime athletic and academic commitments have lessened. The client reports that she is happy to be out of school and spoke again about not fitting in with her peers. She states that there are limited opportunities for sustaining friendships and worries that she will never find a romantic interest. She reports that her mother has suspended her social media account because the client was overly consumed by the number of "likes" that she received for her online posts. You explain that you will be starting a 12-week group of diverse teens who also experience anxiety and would like her to join. She agrees and is eager to participate.

7. You are concerned about the client's online activity. You search and find her social media account, view the content, and find evidence of cyberbullying. You and your supervisor use an ethical decision-making model to appropriately determine which of the following?

- a. You must breach confidentiality and inform the client's parents
- b. You must disclose the findings to the client and assess for safety
- c. You must respect the client's privacy unless she permits you to view her social media account
- d. You must respect the client's privacy but report the cyberbullying peers

8. The preaffiliation, or forming, stage of group development is characterized by which of the following?

- a. Separation
- b. Dependency and inclusion
- c. Power and control
- d. Structure and trust

9. Your responsibility as the group leader is to establish group rules, set limits, and develop a plan for group termination. In doing so, which leadership skill are you exhibiting?

- a. Fostering autonomy
- b. Meaning attribution
- c. Executive functioning
- d. Emotional stimulation

PART THREE

SECOND SESSION, 12 WEEKS AFTER THE INITIAL INTAKE

The client attends group therapy and is making therapeutic gains. Her overall anxiety has decreased, and she is engaging in more constructive thinking. Today is week 6 out of the 12 scheduled weekly group sessions. The client continues to work on increasing her assertiveness and has become less tentative with self-disclosures. She is pleasant and cooperative but remains eager to please others. Three group participants have formed a subgroup (i.e., clique) and have excluded others. The client has begun to take social risks, and today she shares about a time when she felt most anxious. You notice the subgroup whispering and laughing after her disclosure. She nervously turns to you to gauge your response.

10. You feel protective of the client and find yourself becoming increasingly angry with the subgroup's negative behavior. What is the likely source of these feelings?

    a. Countertransference
    b. Transference
    c. Unhealthy group dynamics
    d. Underdeveloped leadership skills

11. Three of the subgroup participants are exhibiting negative behaviors. Which one of the following observations would most likely indicate that the client's group has successfully moved on to the next stage of development?

    a. Avoidance of controversy
    b. Group momentum slows down
    c. Acceptance of all group members
    d. Members vying for leadership roles

12. How should you respond to the negative interactions between the client and the members of the subgroup?

    a. Block the negative behavior and reestablish protective norms.
    b. Evoke universality by asking the client to share how the experience has made her feel.
    c. Use linking to help the client recognize similar feelings that she experienced in her past.
    d. Impart information by offering your interpretation of the interaction.

13. Your time-limited group is coming to an end. During this final phase, you and the group members process key elements EXCEPT which of the following?

    a. Identifying individual changes in anxiety-related beliefs, attitudes, and behaviors
    b. Resolving any conflicted relationships
    c. Generalizing the skills learned in group
    d. Identifying members in need of a future "booster" session

Case Study 6

PART ONE

INTAKE

<u>CLIENT</u>

Age: 74

Sex: Female

Gender: Female

Sexuality: Heterosexual

Ethnicity: Caucasian

Relationship Status: Divorced

Counseling Setting: Community Mental Health Center

Type of Counseling: Individual and psychoeducation

Presenting Problem: Memory impairment

Diagnosis: Mild Neurocognitive Disorder (MND) Unspecified with Behavioral Disturbance (apathy and mood disturbance) 799.59 (R41.9)

<u>PRESENTING PROBLEM:</u>

You work in a mental health center and are conducting an initial assessment on a 74-year-old Caucasian female. The client and her daughter arrive today with a copy of the client's recent neuropsychological evaluation. The evaluation shows cognitive functioning deficits, and the neuropsychologist has diagnosed the client with mild neurocognitive disorder (MND). The client and her daughter fear that her memory issues could worsen and impact her independence. The daughter has seen a gradual decline in the client's memory, which coincides with episodes of depression. The client expresses embarrassment over her memory issues and states, "remembering the simplest things—like doctor's appointments or paying bills—has started to become more and more difficult." She states that she no longer participates in things she once enjoyed, including her book club, church services, and fitness classes.

<u>MENTAL STATUS EXAM:</u>

The client is appropriately dressed and cooperative. She is tearful at times and often glances over at her daughter when she is unsure of how to respond to a question. The client denies suicidal and homicidal ideations. She is oriented to the day, month, and year, but she could not recall the date or place. She recalls the city with prompting. The client's sleep is fair, and her appetite is normal. She reports feeling sad most of the day, every day. To date, medical procedures used to determine the etiology of the client's cognitive impairment have been inconclusive. She awaits an appointment for a positron emission tomography (PET) scan, which can help determine the presence of brain activity associated with Alzheimer's disease. She denies substance use and says that she is a social drinker. Her judgment and awareness are fair, and she denies audio and visual hallucinations.

<u>FAMILY AND WORK HISTORY:</u>

The client divorced nearly 15 years ago and has lived alone since. She has two adult children and four grandchildren who all live locally. She reports experiencing depression and anxiety for most of her life. She currently takes an antidepressant and has done so for years. The client's career was in school administration, where she dedicated nearly 30 years of service until retiring 6 years ago. She reports that retirement caused an increase in depression as she grieved the "loss of (her) identity." The client's mother had Alzheimer's disease, which placed significant stress on the client and her father. The client's sister is diagnosed with bipolar disorder, and there are no other noted mental health or substance use disorders in the family.

1. Which screening and assessment instrument includes the question, "What are the three objects that I asked you to remember a few moments ago?"

    a. Cornell Scale for Depression in Dementia (CSDD)
    b. Vineland-II
    c. Daily Living Activities 20 (DLA-20)
    d. Mini-Mental State Examination (MMSE)

2. Which one of the following is true of individuals with mild neurocognitive disorder?

    a. Cognitive deficits interfere with activities of daily living (i.e., bathing, dressing).
    b. Cognitive deficits interfere with successfully completing tasks such as paying bills and other complex instrumental activities.
    c. Cognitive deficits do not interfere with the capacity for independence.
    d. Cognitive deficits occur exclusively in the context of delirium.

3. You assess for disturbances in social cognition, which is indicated by several symptoms or observations EXCEPT which of the following?

    a. Diminished motivation in pursuing hobbies
    b. Difficulty remembering social cues
    c. Increased introversion
    d. Difficulty remembering names of acquaintances

4. Which one of the following statements reflects a person-centered approach to the client's retirement?

    a. "You have a deep conviction that some of your best years were before retirement."
    b. "Your heart is heavy after leaving a career that was once everything to you."
    c. "Your sadness and the person you are today are likely the results of unconscious processes."
    d. "You're grieving a heavy loss. How does that affect your present-day, here-and-now experiences?"

5. You are a certified counselor who has never worked with a client diagnosed with MND. You assess your ability to work with this client based on your credentials and the information provided thus far. At this point in treatment, which of the following statements is the most accurate?

    a. Your background and training should permit you to work with this client.
    b. You should refer the client to a counselor who specializes in neurocognitive disorders.
    c. You should proceed with the client only after obtaining specialized training and consultation.
    d. You should proceed with the client unless the results of the PET scan indicate advanced memory impairment.

6. The client's neuropsychological testing scores on a normal distribution place her one standard deviation below the mean. The client scored as well as or better than approximately what percent of the normed population?

    a. 3%
    b. 16%
    c. 48%
    d. 85%

7. How can you best engage the client and her daughter in the early stages of treatment?

    a. Normalizing feelings associated with the aging process
    b. Summarizing key concerns and identified areas of focus
    c. Constructing a multigenerational genogram
    d. Advising against "catastrophizing" and "negative predictions"

PART TWO
FIRST SESSION, 6 WEEKS AFTER THE INITIAL INTAKE

The client presents today with a blunted affect and an irritable mood. The daughter accompanies the client and states that the results of the client's recent PET scan show changes in the brain that may indicate Alzheimer's disease. You process the results with the client and her daughter and provide psychoeducation on cognitive impairment, including counseling risks, benefits, and limitations. The client would like to focus on improving psychosocial issues associated with her cognitive impairment.

8. Which of the following psychosocial interventions uses tangible memory triggers to prompt discussions of past experiences?

    a. Validation therapy
    b. Reminiscence therapy
    c. Cognitive stimulation therapy
    d. Reality orientation

9. You ask the client to share her previous experiences participating in her church, book club, and fitness classes. What are you trying to accomplish?

    a. Determine the client's level of cognitive functioning before she discontinued these activities.
    b. Assess individualized belief systems that may interfere with adherence to counseling.
    c. Underscore the value of renewing and maintaining social support and exercise.
    d. Identify any interpersonal stressors or trauma that caused her to discontinue these activities.

10. The client states, "People must think I'm so stupid when I can't even remember whether or not I paid a bill." You respond, "You feel embarrassed when you are unable to complete a task that you used to do with ease." This is an example of which of the following?

    a. Paraphrasing
    b. Attending
    c. Reframing
    d. Empathetic reflecting

PART THREE
SECOND SESSION, 12 WEEKS AFTER THE INITIAL INTAKE

You are on maternity leave, and your supervisor is covering your cases while you are out of the office. The supervisor meets with the client and daughter for the first time today and discusses the client's progress and her treatment plan goals. The client and her daughter report measurable improvements with symptoms of depression and apathy. During today's session, the supervisor also learns that you and the daughter went to high school together and share multiple acquaintances. There is no documentation in the client's chart indicating that the risks and benefits of multiple relationships were reviewed with the client. At the end of the session, the supervisor asks the client for her copay. The daughter and the client state that you have "always just waived the copay," indicating that the final bill would eventually be "written off by the agency."

11. When considering the risks and benefits of multiple relationships, counselors must take appropriate professional precautions. Which of the following is NOT a professional precaution that counselors must take when engaging in multiple relationships?
- a. Informed consent
- b. Signed waivers
- c. Documentation
- d. Supervision

12. Which of the following statements best reflects the supervisor and counselor's ethical responsibility for collecting the client's agreed-upon fees (i.e., copays)?
- a. Waiving copays is permissible when it contributes to the public good (*pro bono publico*).
- b. Waiving copays is permissible only if a predetermined fee-splitting contract exists between the counselor and the supervisor.
- c. Collecting copays through a collection agency is permissible if the client was originally informed of this possibility and previous efforts were made to collect copays.
- d. Collecting copays is not permissible because there was a verbal agreement that the fees would be "written off."

13. The client has met her goals for reducing symptoms of depression and apathy; however, her memory has not improved. How should you proceed?
- a. Discuss termination due to the client meeting her goals related to depression and apathy.
- b. Discuss referring the client to another professional who can address her memory impairment.
- c. Continue to work with the client and create treatment plan goals addressing memory impairment.
- d. Continue to work with the client and renew treatment plan goals for depression and apathy.

Case Study 7

PART ONE
INTAKE
CLIENT
Age: 30

Sex: Female

Gender: Female

Sexuality: Heterosexual

Ethnicity: Caucasian

Relationship Status: Single

Counseling Setting: Agency

Type of Counseling: Outpatient

Presenting Problem: Recent Hospital Discharge

Diagnosis: Borderline Personality Disorder (BPD) 301.83 (F60.3)

PRESENTING PROBLEM:

You are a mental health counselor in an outpatient setting. Your client is a 30-year-old white female who was released from the hospital 48 hours ago. The client presents today for a postdischarge follow-up appointment. The hospital clinician diagnosed the client with borderline personality disorder (BPD) and substance use disorder. The client has a history of suicidality, impulsivity, and relational instability. She explains that she has a "quick temper," which occurs when she is feeling rejected. She explains that she has a long history of being treated poorly by others, including her last boyfriend, former employers, and family members. During these times, the client admits to substance misuse and self-mutilation (i.e., cutting). She states that there are times when she drinks to black out and that she is more inclined to do so when her feelings become intolerable. The client has had multiple hospital admissions and has been in the care of several counselors. She questions your credentials and your ability to "work with someone like (her)."

MENTAL STATUS EXAM:

The client is wearing a low-cut blouse and short shorts. Her affect and mood are labile, and her speech is pressured. She is fidgety at times and sits with her arms crossed. The client states that she has had three previous suicide attempts and has been cutting since her late twenties. Her last suicide attempt was an overdose, which resulted in her recent hospitalization. She stated that this was the result of her last boyfriend "ghosting" her. The client denies audiovisual hallucinations but states that she often feels that others are conspiring against her. She says that she continues to have suicidal thoughts but denies having a current plan.

FAMILY AND WORK HISTORY:

The client attended 3 years of college and reports dropping out due to "depression, anxiety, and anger issues." She has worked off and on as a server at several restaurants and says she usually quits after coworkers or employers "reject or betray her." The client's mother was a teenager when the client was born. Her mother is diagnosed with bipolar disorder, which first appeared after childbirth. She reports moving back and forth between caretakers when she was younger. Her maternal grandmother eventually became her legal guardian and died when the client was in her early twenties. The client reports that she constantly fears abandonment and has "never been successful in a relationship." She has limited contact with her mother, and the identity of her father is unknown.

1. Borderline personality disorder (BPD) is clustered with similar personality disorders characterized by which of the following traits?
   a. Odd or eccentric behavior
   b. Fearful thinking and impulsive behavior
   c. Dramatic and overly emotional behavior
   d. Acute mood lability and social isolation

2. The client experiences multiple symptoms indicative of BPD EXCEPT which of the following?
   a. Fear of abandonment
   b. Suicidality
   c. Intense anger
   d. Grandiosity

3. After reviewing the client's hospital records, you conduct an unstructured interview to confirm and retain the diagnosis of substance use disorder. Your clinical judgment may have been influenced by which of the following?
   a. Confirmation bias
   b. Overconfidence bias
   c. Affect heuristic
   d. The Hawthorne effect

4. The client is wearing a low-cut blouse and short shorts while stating that she attempted suicide due to her last boyfriend "ghosting" her. Carl Jung would most likely view this as an expression of which one of the following?
   a. Persona
   b. Electra complex
   c. Anima
   d. Parapraxis

5. Which one of the following is more indicative of suicidal self-injury than nonsuicidal self-injury (NSSI)?
   a. Difficulty coping with negative emotions and poor self-worth immediately before the injurious act
   b. A persistent urge to cause harm that is often difficult to resist
   c. A desire to cause harm, to feel better, or to end distressing feelings permanently
   d. The constant need to regulate persistent emotional pain and self-critical thoughts

6. To help improve your clinical judgment, your supervisor suggests that you first rule out a substance use disorder diagnosis by using a standardized instrument. Which instrument provides a screening component followed by an assessment for those who screen positive?

   a. CRAFFT (car, relax, alone, forget, friends, trouble) screening test
   b. CAGE (cut down, annoyed, guilty, and eye-opener) questionnaire
   c. MAST (Michigan Alcohol Screening Test)
   d. TAPS (Tobacco, Alcohol, Prescription Medication, and other Substance use) tool

PART TWO

FIRST SESSION, 2 WEEKS AFTER THE INITIAL INTAKE:

You and the client develop a clear and explicit treatment contract to provide a foundation for informed consent. Through this collaborative process, you establish an agreement outlining treatment roles, responsibilities, and expectations for you and the client. The client agrees with your suggested goals but does not want to include safety issues as part of her treatment plan. You provide psychoeducation on BPD, and she relates to experiences of abandonment. She would like to learn how to navigate romantic relationships and requests interventions targeting this area.

7. What is the primary purpose for engaging the client in the process of contract setting?

   a. To establish trust and build a working alliance
   b. To eliminate client "splitting" and manipulation
   c. To provide legal protection in the event of a boundary violation
   d. To give grounds for termination if the client does not uphold her portion of the agreement

8. Which ethical principle would best guide your response to the client's request to exclude safety issues from her treatment plan?

   a. Veracity
   b. Justice
   c. Autonomy
   d. Beneficence

9. To address the client's desire for successful intimate relationships, you select an approach that uses a process known as "limited reparenting" as a means for helping the client form more secure attachments. Which of the following interventions makes use of limited reparenting?

   a. Transference-focused psychotherapy
   b. Schema-focused therapy
   c. Dialectical behavioral therapy
   d. Mentalization-based treatment

PART THREE

SECOND SESSION, 4 WEEKS AFTER THE INITIAL INTAKE:

The client no-showed for her last session without calling to cancel. She arrives today, appearing disheveled and irritable. The client states that she has not been sleeping well. She explains that she was talking to someone on an online dating site and had planned a face-to-face meeting this past weekend. She says she waited at the bar for more than an hour and finally realized that her date had stood her up. She explained that she was in so much shame after the incident that she engaged in self-harm. The client reveals superficial razor cuts on her thigh and upper arm. She says she feels like she is a failure and undeserving of love.

10. You ask the client to relax into the present moment and acknowledge thoughts and feelings that may arise without categorizing them as good or bad. Why are you engaging the client in this exercise?

    a. To identify core beliefs
    b. To teach conflict resolution skills
    c. To assess the client's capacity for transference
    d. To encourage a nonjudgmental stance

11. You model a dialectical stance for the client by providing acceptance while simultaneously facilitating change. This is a process known as which of the following?

    a. Validation
    b. Affirmation
    c. Confirmation
    d. Clarification

12. The client has difficulty identifying and differentiating overwhelming emotions. What technique could help her experience gradations of feeling?

    a. Escalation point recognition
    b. Mood monitoring
    c. Affect labeling
    d. Cue identification

13. How might a gestalt therapist respond to the client's resistance to change?

    a. Identify the client's boundary disturbances.
    b. Engage the client in forceful disputing.
    c. Analyze the client's life scripts.
    d. Roll with the client's resistance.

Case Study 8

PART ONE

INTAKE

<u>CLIENT</u>

Age: 41

Sex: Female

Gender: Female

Sexuality: Heterosexual

Ethnicity: Caucasian

Relationship Status: Divorced

Counseling Setting: Behavioral Health

Type of Counseling: Outpatient

Presenting Problem: Fear and Panic

Diagnosis: Agoraphobia 300.22 (F40.00)

PRESENTING PROBLEM:

You work in a behavioral health outpatient center. Your client is a 41-year-old Caucasian female presenting with symptoms of fear and panic. The client has a history of anxiety and depression but explains that her anxiety has worsened within the last year and that she has begun to experience panic attacks. She states that she has an "overwhelming fear" of elevators and stairwells. When exposed to these situations, she has trouble breathing, begins to feel dizzy, and hyperventilates. The client remembers having her first panic attack while staying at a hotel one weekend. She was taking the stairs and suddenly felt intense fear and panic. On the same trip, she had a similar experience when taking the elevator. The client quit her last job due to travel requirements, and she is currently unemployed. She stays away from stairwells and elevators as much as she possibly can. When unable to do so, she asks her son to accompany her.

MENTAL STATUS EXAM:

The client appears her stated age, and she is dressed in casual attire. Her affect and mood are anxious. She is tearful and seems extremely distressed when recounting her panic attacks. The client denies suicidal or homicidal ideations but does endorse feeling hopeless about her condition. She is unsure if she will benefit from counseling and expresses mixed feelings about seeking help. The client denies audio and visual hallucinations.

FAMILY AND WORK HISTORY:

The client was married for 15 years before she divorced. She and her ex-husband share custody of their 16-year-old son. The client is an only child and reports that her parents were strict and overbearing when she was growing up. She works as a travel photographer and, until recently, worked for a large national publication. She enjoyed her job but cannot envision a time when she would feel comfortable staying in hotels again. This fear has prevented her from exploring other travel accommodations while on assignment. She states, "There are too many unknowns with travel, and I just don't think I can do it any longer."

1. Which one of the following DSM-5 criteria is indicative of agoraphobia?

    a. Fear of being separated from an attachment figure
    b. Fear of being judged in social situations
    c. Fear of being trapped in situations in which escape is perceived as unlikely
    d. Fear of parting with possessions despite excessive acquisition or clutter

2. Which of the following is a risk and prognostic factor for agoraphobia?

    a. Negative events in childhood (e.g., separation, death of a parent)
    b. Serious social neglect
    c. Interpersonal physical and sexual abuse
    d. Neglect and/or lack of supervision

3. You use a biopsychosocial assessment during the client's initial intake appointment. Which one of the following uses a holistic approach to address a client's biopsychosocial and spiritual dimensions?

    a. Cognitive-behavioral
    b. Humanistic
    c. Psychoanalytic
    d. Behavioral

4. You are using the transtheoretical model of change (Prochaska & DiClemente, 1992) to examine the client's reticence to participate in counseling. This model suggests that change is least likely to occur in which of the following stages:

    a. Preparation
    b. Action
    c. Maintenance
    d. Contemplation

5. The client's insurance company is requesting a level-of-care assessment. In behavioral health settings, which of the following would best help with this determination?

    a. Medical necessity
    b. Diagnosis
    c. Treatment summary
    d. Payor source

6. The client relies on her son when she is too anxious to leave the house, and she describes her parents as overbearing. How might a structural family therapist define the boundaries in the client's family?

    a. Flexible
    b. Clear
    c. Disengaged
    d. Diffuse

PART TWO
FIRST SESSION, 2 WEEKS AFTER THE INITIAL INTAKE

The client receives psychoeducation on various treatment interventions for agoraphobia. She understands the risks and benefits, and you review informed consent each session. The client would like to work on her fear of stairs first, which is less anxiety-provoking than elevators. She expresses an understanding of exposure exercises and is willing to give them a try. You and the client use a Subjective Units of Distress Scale (SUDs) to measure the intensity of each anxiety-provoking situation, which can range from 0 units (no distress) to 100 units (extreme distress).

7. Which of the following exposure exercises would be most effective for this client?

    a. Walk up and down the stairs pausing to use relaxation strategies when the SUD rating increases.

    b. Walk up and down the stairs and repeat the exposure until the SUD rating drops by half.

    c. Walk up and down the stairs with her son or a safe person during initial exposures.

    d. Walk up and down the stairs with prescribed antianxiety medication to use PRN.

8. You select interoceptive exposure exercises to address the client's anxiety and panic. How would you tailor this approach to match the client's needs?

    a. Use in vivo exposure by first standing in front of a high-rise building.

    b. Induce dizziness by spinning around in a swivel chair.

    c. Imagine a staircase and vividly recount fear-evoking scenes.

    d. Use virtual reality technology to recreate a computer-generated staircase.

9. Capnometry-assisted respiratory training (CART) is an approach for agoraphobia that targets underlying biological factors. The theoretical framework for CART is based on which of the following assumptions?

    a. Muscle tension resulting from anxiety and panic can be treated with progressive relaxation and deep breathing.

    b. Drops in body temperature resulting from anxiety and panic can serve as an alert to start using coping strategies and deep breathing.

    c. Increased heart rate resulting from anxiety and panic can be altered with autogenic relaxation and mindfulness meditation.

    d. Low levels of carbon dioxide resulting from anxiety and panic can be altered with shallow breathing and a cognitive sense of being in control.

PART THREE

SECOND SESSION, 8 WEEKS AFTER THE INITIAL INTAKE

The client's son accompanies her to her appointment today. Since the initial intake, COVID-19 has become a global pandemic and has greatly impacted the client's anxiety and fear. The client was visibly trembling when she spoke and requested that her son remain nearby. She explained that complying with the statewide mask mandate has been difficult, stating, "Wearing this mask makes me feel like I can't breathe. It's the same feeling I get when I'm walking up stairs or taking the elevator." The client's internist prescribes alprazolam (Xanax), which she has been taking for years. However, she thinks that it is no longer effective and asks if you can help her discontinue the medication. Given the COVID-19 outbreak, you discuss providing distance counseling to the client.

10. How should you respond to the client's request to help her discontinue her alprazolam?

    a. Obtain a signed release for you to speak with her prescribing doctor.

    b. Obtain a signed release to speak to your agency's psychiatrist.

    c. Encourage gradual tapering and monitor any side effects.

    d. Encourage her to follow up with the prescribing doctor.

11. Informed consent for distance counseling addresses issues unique to telehealth EXCEPT which of the following?

    a. Risks and benefits of telehealth
    b. Emergency procedures
    c. Interjurisdictional practice
    d. Time zone differences

12. The American Counseling Association (ACA) Code of Ethics (2014) guidelines for distance counseling, technology, and social media includes which of the following standards?

    a. Counselors verify their identity and the identity of the client (e.g., through the use of code words, numbers) each session.
    b. Counselors take reasonable precautions to ensure the confidentiality of information transmitted through technology-based communication.
    c. Counselors inform clients that only authorized individuals have access to confidential information.
    d. Counselors acknowledge the differences between synchronous and asynchronous communication and use synchronous communication whenever possible to avoid missed verbal and nonverbal cues.

13. You search for randomized clinical trials to determine the efficacy of distance counseling for agoraphobia. Which one of the following best ensures that a study's conclusions are free from bias?

    a. Per-protocol analysis
    b. Transactional analysis
    c. Intention-to-treat analysis
    d. On-treatment analysis

Case Study 9

PART ONE

INTAKE

CLIENT

Age: 7

Grade: 2nd

Sex: Male

Gender: Male

Ethnicity: African American

Counseling Setting: Community Mental Health, School-Based Services

Type of Counseling: Individual and Collateral

Presenting Problem: Impulsivity; Inattention; Hyperactivity

Diagnosis: Attention-Deficit Hyperactivity Disorder (ADHD) 314.01 (F90.2)

PRESENTING PROBLEM:

You are a clinical mental health counselor providing on-site school-based services in a public elementary school. Your client is a 7-year-old African American male enrolled in the 2nd grade. The client is accompanied by his mother, who states that she is here because the school "requested an ADHD assessment." The school reports that the client is disruptive, refuses to follow directions, disturbs others, and has difficulty staying on task. The mother describes the client as "energetic" and "strong-willed"—behaviors that she believes are "just typical for a boy." She is upset that the school wants to conduct a formal evaluation to determine if the client qualifies for a more restrictive classroom setting. The school's population is predominantly white, and the mother believes that her son is being treated unfairly because of his race.

MENTAL STATUS:

The client is dressed appropriately, and he is well groomed. His affect is bright when engaged in an activity of his choice, but he becomes irritable when asked to comply with a direct request (e.g., pick up the toys, walk in the hallway). He is energetic, eager to please, and interrupts your conversation with the mother, as evidenced by the client stating multiple times, "Watch this! Hey! Watch! Look what I can do!" The client has difficulty transitioning from your office and back to his classroom. He runs ahead of you in the hallway and does not respond to redirection. The client has not voiced suicidal or homicidal ideation.

DEVELOPMENTAL AND FAMILY HISTORY:

The client's mother and father are married, and the client has a sister who is 3 years old. The mother denies drug or alcohol use during pregnancy. She is a smoker but states that she cut down when she discovered she was pregnant with the client. The client was delivered at 34 weeks and weighed 5 pounds and 6 ounces. He stayed in the newborn intensive care unit for 10 days after delivery. The client was toilet trained at 24 months, walked at 12 months, and talked at 18 months. The client's paternal grandmother has been treated for bipolar disorder. His maternal uncle has a history of substance abuse, which his mother cites as the reason why she is opposed to the client going on medication.

1. ADHD is grouped under which DSM-5 classification?

  a. Impulse-control disorders
  b. Neurodevelopmental disorders
  c. Disruptive disorders
  d. Social engagement disorders

2. Which of the following conditions is more likely to co-occur with ADHD?

  a. Oppositional defiant disorder
  b. Social anxiety disorder
  c. Intermittent explosive disorder
  d. Major depressive disorder

3. You would like to use ADHD interventions consistent with evidence-based practices (EBP). Components of EBP include all of the following EXCEPT

  a. The clinician's knowledge, skills, and expertise
  b. The client's culture, preferences, and values
  c. Cost-effectiveness and duration of treatment
  d. Research evidence with the least probability of bias

4. According to Jean Piaget, the client's thinking can be characterized by which one of the following?

  a. Uses deductive reasoning and logic
  b. The ability to understand abstract ideas
  c. Thinks concretely and begins to perform logical operations
  d. Can think about what-if or hypothetical situations

5. You find several ADHD interventions consistent with EBP and would like to narrow down your search. Research methodologies with the highest level of evidence include which of the following?

  a. Correlational research designs
  b. Quasiexperimental studies
  c. Randomized control trials
  d. Ex post facto designs

6. Which one of the following assessment instruments provides ADHD rating scales for parents and teachers?

  a. ADHD Rating Scale-IV (ADHD-RS-IV) with Adult Prompts
  b. Conners Rating Scale (CRS)
  c. Woodcock-Johnson IV (WJ IV)
  d. Ages and Stages Questionnaire (ASQ)

PART TWO

FIRST SESSION, 4 WEEKS AFTER THE INITIAL INTAKE

You have been working with the client weekly and are meeting with the mother today to discuss interventions that she can use at home. She relays that her husband does not support the diagnosis of ADHD and has reached out to their faith community instead. The mother is conflicted about counseling and explains that it is viewed as a sign of weakness in her community. She continues to voice concern over the school's lack of diversity and her belief that the client is being treated differently because of his race.

7. Which of the following would help you engage the client's mother in treatment?

    a. Refute the core cultural beliefs surrounding mental health stigma.
    b. Recognize the impact of the intersectional contexts of privilege and marginalization.
    c. Explore the influence of her biases toward the school's majority culture.
    d. Denote the incongruence between historical trauma and here-and-now experiences.

8. In a research study, which methodological feature considers ethnocultural variables when determining external validity?

    a. Design of the study
    b. Choice of outcome measures
    c. Length of follow-up
    d. Criteria for inclusion-exclusion

9. Which statement accurately reflects the ACA Code of Ethics guideline for working with culturally diverse populations?

    a. Counselors recognize existing historical and social prejudices in the misdiagnosis and pathologizing of certain individuals.
    b. Counselors practice only within the boundaries of their competence based on their education, experience, and ability to engage with diverse client populations.
    c. Counselors consider the client's cultural background when providing assessment results and only use bias-free instruments.
    d. Counselors seek supervision when they are at risk of a client imposing their values, attitudes, beliefs, and behaviors onto the counselor.

PART THREE
SECOND SESSION, 6 WEEKS AFTER THE INITIAL INTAKE

You meet with the client's mother today to update the client's treatment plan. Since the beginning of the school year, the client has been suspended for a combined total of 8 days. He has responded poorly to many of the behavioral classroom interventions. The mother has reluctantly granted the school permission to begin testing to determine if the client qualifies for an Individualized Education Program. You inform the mother of her parental rights pertaining to this process, particularly as they apply to protections against disability-related discrimination and the maximum number of disability-related suspensions. She is encouraged by the possibility of the client receiving additional supports that consider the client's strengths and challenges.

10. Federal law requires that an evaluation for an Individualized Education Program be conducted in a nondiscriminatory fashion, and, if qualifications are met, students are entitled to a free and appropriate public education. Which federal law grants this protection?

    a. The United States Civil Rights Law
    b. The Individuals with Disabilities Education Act
    c. The Special Education and Rehabilitative Services Act
    d. The Family Educational Rights and Privacy Act of 1974 (FERPA)

11. The mother reports that she has tried to use planned ignoring when the client interrupts but reports that this behavior has actually worsened. This is likely attributed to which of the following?

    a. Extinction burst
    b. Behavioral activation
    c. Negative reinforcement
    d. Response cost

12. You teach the mother to use time-out with the client at home. The effectiveness of time-out is a function of which one of the following?

    a. Operant conditioning
    b. Classical conditioning
    c. Punishment
    d. Counterconditioning

13. Behavior management for ADHD is grounded in contingency theory and social learning theory. Which of the following is a component of social learning theory?

    a. Discrete trial training
    b. Counterconditioning
    c. Modeling
    d. Differential reinforcement

Case Study 10

PART ONE

INTAKE

<u>CLIENT</u>

Age: 27

Sex: Female

Gender: Female

Sexual Orientation: Heterosexual

Ethnicity: Caucasian

Relationship Status: Married

Counseling Setting: Career Counseling Center

Type of Counseling: Individual

Presenting Problem: Employment-related Stress; Anxiety

Diagnosis: Adjustment Disorder with Anxiety 309.24 (F43.22)

<u>PRESENTING PROBLEM:</u>

You work in a career counseling center, and your intake is a 27-year-old white female employed as a fourth-grade elementary schoolteacher. The client has been a teacher for 3.5 years and has become increasingly dissatisfied with her job. The client explains that she is "at her breaking point" and relays that her stress level has increased sharply within the past 3 months. This is her first school year with a newly hired principal who has been "unreasonably demanding and unsupportive." The client states that she was already second-guessing her career choice and explains that disruptive students and a lack of parental involvement have made teaching incredibly challenging. She reports "stress-induced physical symptoms," which include acute stomach distress and chronic headaches. She worries that her skill set is nontransferable.

<u>MENTAL STATUS:</u>

The client was well-groomed and dressed appropriately. She appears nervous and jittery and quickly places her hands under the table when she notices them shaking. The client states that she is not sleeping well and says it is difficult making it to work each day knowing that "things rarely go as planned." She explains that she has irritable bowel syndrome, which is exacerbated by stress. The client reports that there are no known medical conditions that would cause her chronic headaches. The client denies homicidal or suicidal ideations but remarks that she has felt like this in the past.

<u>WORK AND FAMILY HISTORY:</u>

The client obtained her bachelor's degree in teaching and is currently a certified teacher. She comes from a family of educators, with her mother working as a teacher and her father as a high school guidance counselor. Before college graduation, she worked odd jobs, including waiting tables and working in a public library with preschool groups. She remembers enjoying her student teaching position but states that the class was "nothing like" what she has now. She explains that her student-teaching classroom contained 16 students and that she now struggles to stay on top of her current class of 24. She plays on a tennis team and serves as a "big sister" to a child through a local nonprofit organization. The client is married, and she and her husband do not have children. She reports that her husband has a high-stress job working as an attorney. The client says that he has "little patience with me when I complain about my job stress."

1. In the DSM-5, which of the following is considered "the essential feature" of adjustment disorders?

    a. Emotional or physical symptoms in response to an identifiable stressor
    b. Emotional or cognitive symptoms in response to an identifiable stressor
    c. Emotional or behavioral symptoms in response to an identifiable stressor
    d. Emotional or physiological symptoms in response to an identifiable stressor

2. Adjustment disorders are associated with an increased risk of which of the following?

    a. Completed suicide
    b. Poor concentration
    c. Drug and alcohol misuse
    d. Panic attacks

3. Which theorist would stress the importance of the client's life roles (e.g., tennis player, wife, youth mentor), self-concept, and career maturity?

    a. Hansen
    b. Super
    c. Roe
    d. Schein

4. Which mindfulness-based theory would help the client become more actively involved in values-related activities (e.g., playing tennis or volunteering as a "big sister")?

    a. Reality therapy
    b. Narrative therapy
    c. Adlerian therapy
    d. Acceptance and commitment therapy

5. You would like your treatment goals to reflect elements of John Krumboltz's learning theory of career counseling. Which assessment instrument would help you accomplish this?

    a. Vocational Preference Inventory
    b. Career Orientations Inventory
    c. Vocational Interest Inventory
    d. Career Beliefs Inventory

6. You ask the client to tell you about a time when her problem did not exist or was less severe. Which one of the following approaches reflects this stance?

    a. Freudian psychoanalysis
    b. Solution-focused brief therapy
    c. Transactional analysis
    d. Gestalt therapy

PART TWO

FIRST SESSION, 3 WEEKS AFTER THE INITIAL INTAKE

The client reports that her husband's patience continues to wear thin, so she has explored the possibility of alternate employment. She states that she applied for a position as a curriculum sales representative but did not get an interview. The client reports that the company used a personality inventory to prescreen job applicants. She says that someone in human resources told her she was not selected for an interview because the company was looking for someone who was more extraverted and a "thinker" rather than a "feeler." The client explains that she was under the impression that they were looking for a male. She expresses an interest in using personality inventories to help identify employment that would be a good fit for her.

7. Which is NOT true of the legal and ethical considerations for using personality inventories to conduct preemployment screening?

    a.   Unless the employer can prove otherwise, using personality inventories can violate antidiscrimination laws for people belonging to certain groups (e.g., sex, race).

    b.   The Age Discrimination in Employment Act prohibits preemployment screening instruments from being used as a means for discriminating against those age 50 or over.

    c.   Interpretation and feedback for specific personality inventories must allow questions and clarification and avoid biased terms indicating that a particular personality preference is "not desirable."

    d.   The reliability, validity, and psychometric limitations and appropriateness of instruments must be considered when selecting assessments for preemployment screening.

8. Which of the following personality inventories is based on Carl Jung's theory of psychological types?

    a.   Myers-Briggs Type Indicator

    b.   Strong Interest Inventory

    c.   Career Orientations Inventory

    d.   Ashland Interest Inventory

9. You administer the Self-Directed Search (SDS) career assessment tool to determine the client's three-point Holland code. If the client's code is SAE, which occupation would give her the highest job satisfaction?

    a.   Accountant

    b.   Veterinarian

    c.   Interior decorator

    d.   Systems analyst

10. Which one of the following theories would best address the client's anxiety related to her professional identity and the search for purpose and meaning in her life?

    a.   Existential therapy

    b.   Behavior modification

    c.   CBT

    d.   Psychoanalytic theory

PART THREE

SECOND SESSION, 7 WEEKS AFTER THE INITIAL INTAKE

The client reports that she and her husband have separated and she is now living with her parents. She is tearful and says that the past few days have been challenging. She reports an increase in headaches and stomachaches. The client has interviewed for a teaching position at a private school but doesn't think she can afford a pay cut. Nevertheless, the client continues to be motivated to continue with counseling and believes that she will find a good career fit, but it may take some time. You discuss using a cognitive information processing approach with the client, and she is receptive. You explain that this approach will enable you to examine the communication, analysis, synthesis, valuing, and execution (CASVE) cycle of career decision-making skills.

11. How would you use core counseling skills to respond to your client?

    a. "You and your husband are getting a divorce, and you believe this will negatively affect your future career choices."

    b. "Your marriage is in trouble. Let's look at how this will impact your career choices."

    c. "I know how you feel. I also experienced difficult times with my husband. It took a while, but we are best friends now."

    d. "I'm encouraged that you are committed to the process, but I can't help but notice the sadness you are experiencing today."

12. According to Nancy Schlossberg's adult career development transitions model, which of the following is the client currently experiencing?

    a. An expected transition

    b. An unexpected transition

    c. A chronic transition or chronic "hassles"

    d. A never-occurring transition

13. The client is prioritizing career options and assessing how her choices might impact her community, her significant relationships, and herself. The client is in which of the following CASVE decision-making phases?

    a. Valuing

    b. Analysis

    c. Synthesis

    d. Communication

Case Study 11

PART ONE
INTAKE
CLIENT

Age: 32

Sex: Female

Gender: Female

Sexual Orientation: Heterosexual

Ethnicity: Latina; Mexican American

Relationship Status: Married

Counseling Setting: Community Mental Health

Type of Counseling: Individual and Psychoeducation

Presenting Problem: Depression

Diagnosis: Major Depressive Disorder (MDD) with Psychotic Features 296.24 (F32.3)

PRESENTING PROBLEM:

You work in a community mental health setting. Your client is a 32-year-old Latina presenting with symptoms of depression and psychosis. She reports that she was hospitalized more than 6 months ago and did not attend follow-up appointments due to losing her health insurance coverage. The client currently reports anhedonia, sadness, feelings of worthlessness, and poor concentration. She explains that there are many days when she cannot get out of bed and is unable to fulfill her role as a wife and mother. The client also reports audio hallucinations and says this began when her grandmother died more than a year ago. She explains that her grandmother lived in her home and that her loss was "devastating" to the client. The client is fluent in Spanish and English.

MENTAL STATUS EXAM:

The client is well groomed and appropriately dressed. Her voice is soft and low, and she avoids eye contact, mainly when talking about her family. She states, "I've put them through so much. And I feel so ashamed when I'm unable to care for them." She endorses feelings of hopelessness but denies suicidal and homicidal ideations. The client says that she hears voices and believes that they are the voices of her deceased ancestors trying to communicate with her. She explains that the "spirits" whisper her name in the middle of the night and come to her when she is alone. The client denies command hallucinations. Her appetite is poor, and she has difficulty sleeping "most nights." She has experienced depressive symptoms most of her life, but, outside of the recent hospitalization, she has not sought treatment due to believing that mental illness is a sign of weakness.

HISTORY OF CONDITION AND FAMILY HISTORY:

You obtain a signed release of information before the client's session today, which has enabled you to receive the client's hospital records. The client was admitted due to hallucinations and suicidal ideation. The hospital psychiatrist provided a diagnosis of brief psychotic disorder and bipolar II disorder. The client was prescribed antipsychotic medication and an antidepressant. She reports that she discontinued the antipsychotic medication shortly after discharge because it caused excessive sleepiness. Regarding the antidepressant, the client states, "I just take it on the days when I'm really having a hard time." The client has two teenage sons and lives near her extended family.

1. Of the following, which DSM-5 criteria for MDD can present as delusional?
   a. Excessive or inappropriate guilt
   b. Recurrent thoughts of death
   c. Subjective reports of depression
   d. Estimation of impending danger

2. The client says she felt like her soul left her body upon her grandmother's death. This experience left her with feelings of sadness, loss, worthlessness, and suicidality. This describes which of the following culturally bound conditions?
   a. *Ataque de nervios*
   b. *Confianza*
   c. *Susto*
   d. *Mal de ojo*

3. The DSM-5 Cultural Formulation Interview (CFI) is a clinical assessment tool used to obtain culturally relevant information across all of the following domains EXCEPT:
   a. The cultural definition of the problem
   b. Perception of the problem's cause, context, and support
   c. Experiences of racism and discrimination
   d. Cultural factors affecting current and past help seeking behaviors

4. Although Latinos are multiracial and multicultural, there are some cultural differences between Latinos and Anglo Americans. Which statement accurately depicts these differences?
   a. Latinos place higher importance on their nuclear family than on their extended family.
   b. Latinos are more likely to engage in direct communication than indirect communication (e.g., idioms, metaphors, and stories).
   c. Latinos emphasize personal fulfillment over group (i.e., collective) harmony.
   d. Latinos place greater significance on supernatural forces than on nonspiritual forces.

5. How might you use motivational interviewing to elicit change talk from the client?
   a. Help the client to reevaluate the nature of the relationship with her husband.
   b. Persuade the client to attend a psychiatric evaluation for medication.
   c. Confront the client on how maintaining the status quo is detrimental to progress.
   d. Evoke the client's optimism for change by asking about a previous change she successfully made in her life.

PART TWO
FIRST SESSION, 2 WEEKS AFTER THE INITIAL INTAKE

The client informs you that she is upset because of a recent incident involving her two sons. She states that her teenage sons were walking in a neighborhood park when they came across a group of white men who used xenophobic slurs and threatened them. The boys said the men spit on them and told them to "go back to where they came from." The client's bouts of depression persist, and this is now coupled with the feeling that she has somehow failed to protect her sons. The client is also concerned that her husband is becoming increasingly intolerant of her inability to cook, clean, and care for their boys. The client states this makes her feel "worthless" and a "nobody." She has also become more isolated and misses "having the energy" to connect with those in her community.

6. Which core professional value calls on counselors to promote equity for all people and groups by actively confronting oppressive systems of power?

    a. Professional integrity
    b. Multicultural awareness
    c. Social justice
    d. Beneficence

7. When the client recounts the incident with her two sons in the park, you remain open to the client's underlying experiences in the present moment and respond authentically. This is an example of which one of the following?

    a. Increasing differentiation
    b. Shaping competence
    c. Supplying positive reinforcement
    d. Providing congruence

8. You select Aaron Beck's cognitive model for depression to address the client's feelings of worthlessness. According to Beck, causes of the client's distorted thinking can be attributed to which of the following?

    a. Unresolved unconscious conflicts
    b. Feelings of inferiority due to a mistaken style of life
    c. Activating events, beliefs, and consequences
    d. View of oneself, the world, and one's future

9. You use behavioral activation to help the client with social isolation. Which treatment plan goal reflects this approach?

    a. The client will engage in a minimum of two "values-based" activities each week.
    b. The client will identify two ways of reducing ambivalence and engaging in "change talk."
    c. The client will list a minimum of three faulty assumptions contributing to her "failure identity."
    d. The client will identify at least four individuals who fit into her "quality world."

PART THREE

SECOND SESSION, 12 WEEKS AFTER THE INITIAL INTAKE

The client has been on antidepressants for 3 weeks and has shown improvement with depressive symptoms. She has benefited from weekly counseling sessions and attends a psychoeducational group designed to help reduce stigma associated with mental disorders, provide information on medication management, and improve healthcare access and utilization. It has been 18 months since her grandmother's death, and she has expressed a desire to process feelings of grief and loss.

10. Which approach would help the client understand that depression is an illness (i.e., not a moral failing) stemming from difficult life events (e.g., complicated bereavement)?

    a. Psychoanalytic therapy
    b. Interpersonal therapy
    c. Person-centered therapy
    d. Gestalt therapy

11. The client's religious beliefs and core cultural values are inconsistent with your own worldview. Which theoretical orientation would best provide you with a basis for sound ethical practice?

    a. Behavior therapy
    b. Person-centered therapy
    c. Conversion therapy
    d. Rational-emotive behavioral therapy

12. You help the client process the loss of her grandmother by educating her on Elizabeth Kubler-Ross's stages of grief. Which one of the following accurately depicts this theory?

    a. All cultures experience grief in the same fashion.
    b. Individuals in the first stage of grief may lash out and blame others for their loss.
    c. The stages of grief are often cyclical rather than linear.
    d. In the last stage of grief, individuals experience disbelief, shock, and sadness.

13. Ethical guidelines for the counseling profession state that counselors must refrain from terminating or referring clients based solely on which of the following conditions?

    a. The client's failure to pay agreed-upon fees
    b. The lack of competence required to provide professional assistance
    c. Adherence to personal values, attitudes, beliefs, and behavior
    d. The determination that the client is no longer benefiting from services

Answer Key and Explanations for Test #1

Case Study 1

1. C: Social anxiety disorder is characterized by marked fear or anxiety in social situations and fears of acting in ways that others will scrutinize. According to the DSM-5, "Individuals with social anxiety disorder often have anticipatory anxiety that is focused on upcoming social situations in which they must perform or be evaluated by others" (APA, 2013). This aspect of social anxiety disorder differentiates it from other anxiety disorders. Fear of being incapacitated by an unforeseen panic attack in public is a manifestation of panic disorder. The fear or avoidance of social situations because of perceived appearance-related flaws characterizes body dysmorphic disorder. Individuals with agoraphobia fear not being able to escape certain conditions in the presence of profound anxiety.

2. D: HIPAA protects and safeguards confidential electronic records. Components of the HIPAA Privacy Notice include protecting electronic records from being tampered with, destroyed, or disclosed to unsanctioned persons. The notice further stipulates that protection under HIPAA applies to intentional and unintentional acts. Privilege applies to protecting confidential information in legal proceedings. State and legal mandates dictate information used in court, and mandates vary from state to state. HIPAA is not the same as informed consent. You are not providing consent to treat, nor is the client authorizing information to be released to third parties. HIPAA signatures and initials simply indicate that the client has received or was offered the HIPAA Notice of Privacy Practices. Informed consent (rather than HIPAA) covers the client's rights and responsibilities, including the right to be informed beforehand of privacy and confidentiality policies before consent for treatment is provided.

3. B: The first step in developing self-affirmations is to identify a significant core value. Core values are stable beliefs upon which a person acts or aspires to act. Self-affirmations are used to affirm a person's self-worth. Core values create positive emotional states. Self-affirmation theory is based on the premise that a person's core values provide a more global view of themselves. When self-affirmations are based on core values, the other parts of a person are reinforced and self-concept is better protected. Individuals engaging in self-affirmations are less likely to attribute negative feedback to the current experience and are less likely to distort information. Identifying the activating event is the first step in CBT. Providing the client with unconditional positive regard rather than modeling it is a person-centered technique. Crossed and complementary transactions are concepts associated with transactional analysis.

4. B: The Liebowitz Social Anxiety Rating Scale measures social anxiety; it provides measures for social anxiety and social avoidance, and there are also measures for performance anxiety and performance avoidance. Individuals with performance anxiety may also have negative performance-based appraisals leading to avoidance. Social anxiety disorder characteristics include fear of social situations fueled by cognitive distortions and reinforced by avoidance and other safety behaviors. Cognitive distortions include an underestimation of one's performance in social situations. The Hamilton Anxiety Rating Scale is useful for measuring traits associated with GAD, including psychological distress and somatic complaints. The Beck Anxiety Inventory measures the severity of anxiety symptoms, specifically physiological and cognitive symptoms of anxiety. The Fear Questionnaire Social Phobia Subscale assesses the severity of specific phobias by focusing primarily on avoidance behaviors.

5. D: Stating "This way of decreasing anxiety seems foreign to you" would best increase compliance with engaging in the self-affirmation exercise. Rolling with resistance is a motivational interviewing strategy used to improve a client's desire to change. Statements that focus on the problem and not the person are used when rolling with resistance. The counselor's statement is a simple reflection. The statement "Change is really hard for you, but I think you'll be pleased with the results" focuses on the person rather than the problem and uses persuasion, which motivational interviewing discourages. The statement "There are now studies showing that positive affirmations activate neural reward pathways in the brain" is also an attempt at persuasion. Finally, the statement "You feel as if I don't understand you or can't help you" is a failed attempt at providing empathy because it does not accurately reflect the client's underlying feelings or beliefs.

6. C: Primarily used during the initial stage of group development, the leadership technique of linking best enables members to experience universality. Irvin Yalom (1985) developed the concept of curative factors, also known as therapeutic factors, to encapsulate group member experiences leading to growth. Yalom's curative factors include "altruism, cohesion, universality, interpersonal learning input and output, guidance, catharsis, identification, family reenactment, self-understanding, instillation of hope, and existential factors" (Boon & Vermeiren, 2019). Universality occurs when group members recognize that they have shared experiences, thoughts, and feelings—and that they are not alone. Thus, universality helps validate common experiences and reduce feelings of isolation. Linking is a process used to promote and encourage member-to-member interactions, which help members recognize their similarities and common themes. Facilitating is a basic leadership skill used in the early stages of group therapy to help encourage members to talk to other members rather than the group leader. Interpreting is a leadership skill that relies on a preestablished framework for group therapy (e.g., CBT). Leaders use interpreting to redirect members back to the framework when explaining the meaning of their expressed thoughts and feelings. Confronting is used when counselors find a discrepancy in an element of the client's thoughts, feelings, and actions.

7. D: Gestalt therapists use the term boundary disturbance to describe various forms of resistance. Boundary disturbances include projection, introjection, retroflection, confluence, and deflection. Gestalt therapists address boundary disturbances in the here and now, making it applicable to this client's process-oriented group. Projection is the tendency for a person to blame the environment (i.e., other people) for personality traits, thoughts, feelings, and behaviors that originate in themselves. Individuals use projection to disown or deny aspects of their personality by blaming others for their circumstances. Disowning aspects of one's personality makes the person a victim of circumstance by assigning hidden meanings to others. During group conflict, the member's statement, which consists of personality aspects consistent with social anxiety (i.e., feelings of not being wanted, included, or judged), likely originate in elements of the member's self and other members being in agreement. Introjection, which is the opposite of projection, is the process of assimilating information from the environment without critical discernment. This tends to develop in childhood when information from parents or authority figures is passively incorporated so that there is no identification of what one wants and needs. Deflection occurs when a distraction is created to avoid aspects of the environment that may be threatening. Examples of distractions include the use of humor, speaking for others, and asking questions. Confluence occurs when aspects of one's internal and external environments are blurred or diffuse, which prevents one from differentiating the two. Confluence often occurs when individuals avoid conflict and possess an increased need to be accepted.

8. C: The best response to the group's conflict is the statement, "How might removing a member deprive you of learning from one another?" This question tests your knowledge of the stages of group development, the need to provide a here-and-now focus, and the leadership skills used to promote group cohesion. The middle stage of group development, also appropriately known as the storming stage (Tuckman, 1984), is characterized by conflict among members, challenges toward group leaders, and the formation of alliances or subgroups. Group leaders are tasked with normalizing conflict and redirecting members to here-and-now interpersonal exchanges rather than labeling certain members as "problematic" or "scapegoats." Core beliefs are schemas rooted in childhood. Although counselors can address core beliefs in process-oriented groups, caution must be used when group leaders interpret conflict as core beliefs, partly because it takes away from the group's here-and-now focus. Exploring how members respond to difficult people in their lives is incorrect because it refers to other members as "difficult" rather than ascribing the conflict as member's behaviors.

9. D: Counselors use summarization to tie together certain concepts and themes. Summarization is particularly useful in the middle stages of group development, with special care being taken to emphasize positive growth or therapeutic progress. Genuineness, or congruence, occurs when the counselor's responses are consistent with what the client is expressing. Counselors also use genuineness to show nonjudgmental acceptance, reflect empathetic attunement, and keep the focus on here-and-now interactions. Counselors express unconditional positive regard by showing nonjudgmental acceptance and care for clients. Counselors use empathetic reflection to respond to the client's underlying feelings accurately. Empathetic reflections lead to empathetic responding, which consists of perceiving, understanding, and experiencing what the client is communicating.

10. C: Individuals with anxiety disorder typically try to manage anxiety by engaging in avoidance behaviors, such as not making eye contact or not participating in conversations. Avoidance creates a positive feedback loop that reinforces anxiety and leads to additional self-defeating thoughts and behaviors. Relaxation is not an example of a safety behavior. Relaxation techniques are helpful for the long-term management of anxiety, whereas safety behaviors are not. Safety behaviors are used with and without avoidance behaviors. Safety behaviors include things used to protect individuals from perceived "catastrophic" consequences and include inappropriate giggling or stereotypical movements when performing. Like avoidance behaviors, safety behaviors are not effective for the long-term management of social anxiety. Individuals with social anxiety tend to overestimate rather than underestimate how negatively others judge them. Finally, postevent rumination, a cognitive factor associated with social anxiety, leads to inaccurate evaluations of feared outcomes. Postevent rumination occurs when aspects of the encounter are repeatedly mentally reviewed, thus fueling anxiety and confirming negative perceptions.

11. A: Constructive confrontation is designed to help clients achieve congruence. Humanistic therapists assert that incongruence occurs when there is a discrepancy between clients' perceptions of themselves and reality. Therapists use constructive confrontation when pointing out discrepancies among the client's actions, thoughts, behaviors, perception, or nonverbal communication. An amplified reflection is a motivational interviewing skill used to state the client's original statement and overemphasize their point or intent. Amplified reflections address ambivalence to change, making this answer option incorrect. Attending is the counselor's way of showing interest. The interest can be verbal (e.g., by saying "Go on") or nonverbal (e.g., nodding the head). Finally, counselors use self-disclosure when sharing personal aspects of themselves. Self-disclosure can take many forms and may be appropriate or inappropriate, depending on the counselor's motives (i.e., self-serving versus benefiting the client and/or the therapeutic relationship).

12. A: This is an example of a one-group pretest-posttest experimental design. Pretest-posttest experimental designs are conducted using the following steps: (1) a pretest is administered to a

47

group (e.g., members participating in group therapy for social anxiety), (2) the intervention (e.g., group therapy) is administered, and (3) the same assessment used in the pretest is again administered as a posttest. The purpose of the one-group pretest-posttest design is to determine if the intervention has created a change (i.e., did it lessen social anxiety and the related performance avoidance?). This design limits internal validity because of confounding factors, such as history, maturation, instrument decay, and regression toward the mean. It has no external validity. Group posttest comparison does not include a pretest. Group posttests are administered to a group after an intervention. One advantage of group pretests is randomization, which allows the experimenter to control for maturation and history. The "one-shot" case study is a design in which one group is observed on one occasion after the intervention. This design is limited because there is no control group. Two-group nonrandom-selection pre-test-posttest designs consist of an experimental group and a control group. One group is given a pretest, followed by treatment or intervention, and then a posttest is administered. The control group receives a pretest and a posttest only. This design also has limitations related to nonrandomization, such as selection and maturation.

13. A: The group intervention serves as the independent variable. An independent variable is the variable that the experimenter manipulates. Social performance anxiety serves as the dependent variable. Dependent variables are what is observed or measured as being directly affected by the independent variable. In this scenario, you wish to determine the effectiveness of the group intervention (i.e., the independent variable) on social performance anxiety (i.e., the dependent variable). In this study, you use the same instrument for your pretest and posttest, neither one of which serves as the independent variable.

Case Study 2

1. D: The process of informed consent includes reviewing with the client payment, fees, and insurance benefits, including policies and procedures for nonpayment. Practitioners provide informed consent on an ongoing basis throughout the counseling relationship. Informed consent includes all of the essential information for the client to make an informed decision about receiving services. Other aspects of informed consent include the potential risks and benefits of counseling, emergency procedures, the overall purpose and goals, counselor credentials, and the role of technology. The confidentiality agreement is also part of informed consent. Privacy involves keeping confidential information secure. Therefore, privacy and confidentiality fall under the client's rights and responsibilities section of informed consent. Lastly, an explanation of limitations is part of the confidentiality agreement and refers to informing clients of the circumstances in which a breach of confidentiality may occur.

2. B: Developed for the DSM-5, the CFI is a tool used to collect culturally relevant information related to the client's current and past help-seeking behaviors, coping skills, treatment expectations, and other relevant socially and culturally contextualized factors (Lewis-Fernandez et al., 2020). The Ethnic-Sensitive Inventory (ESI) is a self-assessment questionnaire for counselors and related practitioners that measures counselor-client interactions in four phases of counseling (i.e., from precontact to termination). The Munroe Multicultural Attitude Scale Questionnaire (MASQUE) is a tool that measures multicultural knowledge, care, and active experiences among students attending secondary educational institutions (Monroe & Pearson, 2006). Finally, the Iowa Cultural Understanding Assessment—Client Form is a questionnaire intended to provide feedback on culturally responsive care for clinical and program services.

3. A: The study shows a high proportion of people without depression with low scores. BDI-II scoring is as follows: A score of 0–13 is considered in the minimal range, 14–19 is mild, 20–28 is moderate, and 29–63 is severe. Specificity measures (i.e., the true negative rate) are the proportion of people without depression with a low score on the BDI-II. In other words, a specificity of 84% indicates that 84% of individuals without depression did not score above a cutoff score of 14. This also means that the study yielded few false negatives. The same study yielded a sensitivity score of 88%. A sensitivity score is a true positive rate because 88% of those with depression scored above the cutoff score of 14 on the BDI-II. Probability is unrelated to specificity and sensitivity and is used to determine the likelihood or chance of an event occurring.

4. C: Discovering that the BDI-II was significantly correlated with the PHQ-9 is evidence of convergent validity. Convergent validity is defined as the extent to which a test measures the hypothetical construct (e.g., depression) that it intends to measure. To determine if the BDI-II accurately measures depression, the researcher correlated the measurements with those obtained with the PHQ-9. Predictive validity is when a measurement correlates with another variable that takes place in the future (e.g., individuals who score high on tests measuring the onset of an illness are correlated with those who actually develop an illness). Predictive validity is a form of criterion-related validity because the specified measure accurately predicts scores on a criterion measure. Test-retest reliability occurs when participants partake in the same test twice. Reliability is obtained when a test's stability is proven over time (i.e., the scores from time one and time two are consistent and stable).

5. D: The criteria for PDD criteria include feelings of hopelessness, and the criteria for MDD include feelings of worthlessness or inappropriate guilt. The DSM-5 criteria for PDD includes (in part): "The presence, while depressed, of two (or more) of the following: 1. Poor appetite or overeating. 2. Insomnia or hypersomnia. 3. Low energy or fatigue. 4. Low self-esteem. 5. Poor concentration or difficulty making decisions. 6. Feelings of hopelessness" (APA, 2013). The MDD criteria for adults require at least five of nine qualifying criteria to be present over the course of a two-week period and represent a change in the individual's behavior or functioning from baseline. These include "depressive symptoms, loss of interest/pleasure (one of these first two being required), in addition to weight loss/weight gain (not associated with diet) or a decrease in appetite, insomnia or hypersomnia, psychomotor excitement or delay, constant fatigue, excessive sense of guilt/worthlessness, inability to concentrate, and suicidal ideation/obsession/attempt" (APA, 2013).

6. A: Adlerian therapists emphasize the importance of social connection, asserting that all individuals strive for "superiority," which is achieved through a purposeful, goal-oriented "lifestyle." Adlerian therapists contextualize each client's social and cultural factors, initially shaped by family constellation, including birth order. Adlerians focus on each individual's lifestyle as it is influenced by multiple factors, including systemic racism, gender, religion, and sexual orientation. Adlerian and Freudian therapists are categorized as psychoanalytic, and both emphasize early childhood influences; however, Freudians differ in that they also emphasize unconscious processes whereas Adlerians do not. Gestalt therapists are categorized as experiential or relational. Gestalt therapists stress the integration of mind and body through increased awareness of the present moment. For gestalt therapists, wholeness involves the integration of one's cognitive, emotional, and behavioral factors. As their name suggests, person-centered, or Rogerian, therapists allow the client to become fully functioning in the context of the therapeutic experience. The goal of Rogerian therapy is to facilitate congruence between the client's self-image and idealized self.

7. C: You would first seek to better understand and validate the client's experiences with psychiatric care and consider contextualized factors (e.g., race, gender, ethnicity). For example, researchers suggest that African Americans are more likely to be diagnosed with schizophrenia or psychosis than non-Hispanic whites presenting with the same symptoms. Your client's misdiagnosis likely contributes to medical mistrust and influences his help-seeking behaviors.

Establishing a therapeutic alliance at this juncture is critical. Empathetic listening and validation communicate warmth, positive regard, and affirmation. Emphasizing the importance of honest communication regarding suicidality is more likely to occur within the context of a trusting counselor-client relationship. Providing the client with a written copy of informed consent is appropriate but should not be the first consideration. Lastly, obtaining a signed release of information to communicate with the hospital may be helpful. However, using this as an initial response may communicate to the client that you doubt his experiences.

8. B: Cognitive therapy emphasizes the therapeutic alliance as a vital component for addressing cognitive distortions. Aaron Beck is credited with developing cognitive therapy. This treatment assumes that cognitive distortions result from irrational thinking and posits that depression stems from the client's negative view of themselves, others, and the future (i.e., the cognitive triad). Rational-emotive behavior therapy (REBT) is more directive and relies on the therapist challenging and disputing the client's irrational thoughts. REBT therapists view the importance of unconditional acceptance but believe that emphasizing the therapeutic relationship can impede progress and create dependency. Freud and other psychoanalytic theorists believe that the therapeutic relationship is affected by transference and countertransference. Rather than focus on cognitive distortions, psychanalytic therapists value uncovering unconscious motives and biological drives to increase intellectual and emotional awareness. Person-centered therapy is nondirective and collaborative. Person-centered therapists help clients achieve congruence between their values and their behavior. Cognitive therapists adopt a humanistic approach as a foundation for examining irrational thinking, but person-centered therapists do not explore irrational thinking.

9. B: Cognitive therapists use Socratic questioning to help challenge cognitive distortions and evaluate their automatic thoughts by testing them against sound logic and reasoning. For example, the counselor may ask, "What is the evidence for or against this thought?" The client then learns to recognize automatic thoughts and their associated cognitive distortions independently, which is all part of a process known as cognitive restructuring. Counterconditioning is an unrelated term used by behavioral therapists to refer to an experimental procedure in which a subject is trained to respond to a stimulus incompatible with a previously learned response to the same stimulus. Forceful disputing is a rational-emotive behavioral therapy technique used to challenge irrational thoughts and beliefs. Assuming responsibility is a gestalt therapy technique. Gestalt therapists using this technique ask clients to add the phrase, "and I take responsibility for it," to statements to help promote personal responsibility for their thoughts, actions, and feelings.

10. A: The best way to identify factors affecting the client's clinical presentation and treatment plan goals is to construct a case conceptualization. Cognitive therapists promote the use of biopsychosocial assessments to assist in building a sound clinical presentation. Sperry and Sperry (2020) promote using the eight P's when formulating the client's case conceptualization; these include presentation, predisposition (including culture), precipitants, protective factors and strengths, pattern, perpetuants, (treatment) plan, and prognosis. Summarizing the client's reasons for feeling stuck may help provide context to help understand the client's views of himself, others, and the world; however, this option is incorrect because the client's reasons for feeling stuck serve as the impetus for revisiting and updating the case conceptualization. Although it is also helpful, an interdisciplinary consultation is not the best process because there is no indication that the counselor lacks the skill set. Instead, the need arose due to the client's shift in clinical presentation. The purpose of a functional behavioral analysis is to identify the client's behavioral chain to determine which behaviors are desirable and which ones are undesirable. Once this is determined, the chain can be broken down and areas can be targeted to help lead to an improved outcome. By contrast, the case conceptualization analyzes a wide range of influences that change the client's clinical presentation rather than looking at smaller components leading to behavioral change.

11. B: The client concludes that because he and his girlfriend broke up, he is unworthy of love and is destined to fail romantically; this is an example of overgeneralization, which occurs when broad conclusions are drawn without supporting evidence. Personalization involves a person believing that they are being targeted by someone else's behavior when it has nothing to do with them. Black-and-white, or polarized, thinking consists of "either/or" statements or beliefs. Confirmation bias is the tendency to seek out and retain information in line with one's preconceived notions.

12. A: The downward arrow technique helps facilitate the client's progress by uncovering the client's underlying core beliefs about himself, others, and the world. Core beliefs, generally rooted in childhood experiences, can drive automatic thoughts and lead to distorted thinking. The downward arrow technique identifies the intermediate beliefs impeding progress. The counselor then draws a downward arrow and challenges each rigidly held belief. For example: Client: "I'm destined to fail in all intimate relationships." Counselor: "And what does that mean?" Client: "I'm a failure." Counselor: "If you're a failure, what does that suggest?" Client: "That I'm unlovable." Once the core belief is uncovered, it can be further explored and tested against sound logic and reason. Memory rescripting, or imagery rescripting, is a technique used with clients experiencing flashbacks originating from trauma. The goal of memory rescripting is to alter the memories leading to shame and self-blame. The hidden emotion technique brings to the forefront anxiety-provoking situations that are avoided or denied. Counselors who practice solution-focused therapy use scaling questions to help clients track their progress on an identified goal.

13. C: Cognitive therapists use role reversion to challenge negative cognitions, therefore reducing psychological distress. Role reversion works by instructing clients to switch roles with the counselor and argue against the client's hypothesis associated with distorted thinking. Shame-attacking exercises are REBT techniques designed to be performed in public to reduce the need for others' approval. The theory behind shame-attacking exercises is that by reducing the need for approval, there is also a reduction in catastrophic thinking that fosters feelings of inadequacy. Identifying the three basic musts, or irrational beliefs, is an REBT technique. The three basic musts include (1) believing one must perform in a manner that others affirm or else one is void of self-worth, (2) believing one must be treated in a manner that the client finds affirming or else one is labeled "no good," and (3) believing that one must get what they think they are entitled to or that one's life is unacceptable. Exception questions are a solution-focused technique used to explore times in the client's life when the problem did not exist, thus creating optimism, hope, and the potential for recreating those experiences.

Case Study 3

1. A: Gender identity is a person's conception of being either male, female, or something else. Gender expression is defined as one's outward expression as being either male, female, or something else. Cisgender is the congruence between one's gender identity, gender expression, and gender assigned at birth. Cisgender can be described as a cisgender man or a cisgender woman. Gender dysphoria occurs when there is incongruence between one's experienced/expressed gender and their gender assigned at birth. Gender dysphoria also includes possible destress from the incongruence between one's experienced and assigned genders. All conceptions of gender are culturally determined.

2. C: The DSM-5 defines gender dysphoria as "a marked incongruence between one's experienced/expressed gender and assigned gender." The concept of preferred gender implies that one's gender identity is a choice, which is different than one's experienced gender. Researchers have found that gender identity can be influenced by prenatal factors, including in utero exposure to or absence of exposure to testosterone (Roselli, 2018). Gender reassignment "denotes an official (and usually legal) change of gender" (APA, 2013). Lastly, gender dysphoria involves incongruence between one's assigned gender and one's expressed (rather than suppressed) gender.

3. B: Title IX of the Education Amendments of 1972 prohibits discrimination based on sex in any federally funded educational program (i.e., public schools or state universities). Title IX further defines "sex" to include sexual orientation and gender identity. In 2021, the US Department of Education Office for Civil Rights issued a Title IX Notice of Interpretation, stating that the Department of Education "will enforce Title IX's prohibition on discrimination based on sex to include: (1) discrimination based on sexual orientation and (2) discrimination based on gender identity." Title IX helps ensure that all students experience equity in education. This protection includes allowing students to use gender-neutral restrooms or a restroom that corresponds to their gender identity. FERPA, also known as the Buckley Amendment, protects the privacy of educational records by giving parents the right to access and, if necessary, amend their child's academic records. This same right is given to students 18 and older or students of any age entering postsecondary institutions. Students who wish to change their educational records to reflect their gender identity or name change may be entitled to FERPA protections. Counselors must stay up to date on legislation affecting transgender rights and protections because the scope of these protections varies according to state and federal laws. The First Amendment of the United States Constitution protects freedom of speech. Title II of the ADA protects students with disabilities from discrimination or exclusion from events, services, and programs. Students experiencing gender dysphoria may be protected under ADA or Section 504 if they have a qualifying disability; gender dysphoria itself is not a qualifying disability.

4. D: Bullying is being intentionally aggressive or mean, it is repeated over time, and it involves situations in which there is an imbalance of power. Bullying can occur in a variety of settings, including school, the community, or online. There are various subtypes of bullying, including physical bullying, verbal bullying, relational bullying, and electronic bullying. This differs from teasing and other acts of aggression in that there is an imbalance of power. Power can be physical, social, intellectual, or mental.

5. C: Your best first response is to use self-reflection and self-assessment to examine the personal biases and stereotypes you may have about transgender individuals. Per the ACA Code of Ethics, disclosing your misgivings is unethical because it is not aligned with transaffirmative care and can be detrimental to the client. Conducting a trauma-informed assessment is appropriate, particularly for clients who are at risk for or may have experienced victimization or assault. However, providing this assessment to determine the etiology of the client's gender identity suggests that there is an underlying cause that should be addressed to "fix" or change the "damaged" client. Assessments can be helpful appraisals for gender dysphoria rather than gender identity. Lastly, the ACA Code of Ethics states that counselors must "refrain from referring prospective and current clients based solely on the counselor's personally held values, attitudes, beliefs, and behaviors." It is important to note that, although making values-based referrals is unethical, counselors are ethically responsible for practicing within the boundaries of their professional competence.

6. B: Minority stress theory posits that gender dysphoria is caused not only by external (distal) stressors (e.g., prejudice, discrimination) but also by negatively internalized (proximal) stressors, including internalized transphobia and stigma. Proximal stressors also include anticipated rejection, hiding gender identity out of fear, and the cumulative experiences of being "othered" as a minority in a cisgender culture. Proximal stressors are linked to higher instances of behavioral health disparities and an increase in mental health symptoms. Cognitive dissonance theory asserts that individuals experience distress when faced with two or more incompatible cognitive elements (i.e., choices). Social identity theory explains that individuals are influenced by fitting in and belonging to social groups. Alignment with one's identified social group is likely to affect self-esteem, especially if the identification is strong (i.e., an "in-group" versus an "out-group"). Escape theory states that individuals tend to avoid activities that are psychologically unpleasant.

7. A: Based on the client's diagnosis, an appropriate treatment plan goal would be to reduce distress caused by the desire to identify as another gender. The DSM-5 replaced the term gender identity disorder with gender dysphoria to avoid pathologizing one's identity. Gender expression is defined as the outward expression of one's gender and may or may not align with one's gender identity. Gender identity is defined as one's inner sense of being male, female, a combination of both, or neither. One's gender at birth may or may not coincide with one's gender identity or gender expression. Sexual orientation uncertainty is unrelated to gender dysphoria, making this answer option incorrect. Gender dysphoria is defined as the incongruence between one's expressed or experienced gender and one's assigned gender. Individuals who are nonbinary do not identify as male or female but instead identify as something in between or no gender at all. Cisgender describes individuals whose gender identity is consistent with their birth identity. Reducing incongruence between nonbinary and cisgender identity is not possible because the two are mutually exclusive.

8. B: The primary purpose for collaboration with the client is to validate presenting concerns and establish hope. The therapeutic alliance consists of shared tasks, goals, and bonds (Bordin, 1978). Goals outline agreed-upon measures to alleviate the client's symptoms. Seeking the client's input on these measures helps instill hope and improve confidence in the therapeutic process. Presenting as a united front is incorrect. Although the counselor is an advocate for the client, family sessions value input from all members. Modeling active listening and empathy is not the primary purpose for collaborating with the client. Gaining confidence in self-advocacy is an appropriate treatment plan goal; however, the purpose of collaboration at this time is to strengthen the bond with the client to promote therapeutic change.

9. D: Autonomy is the right of an individual to participate in decisions affecting the direction of their life. Autonomy is an integral part of informed consent. Informed consent is the process by which one understands the benefits and risks of a specific treatment and freely consents to that treatment. Counselors who work with TGNC teens are tasked with providing accurate information on the pros and cons of medical treatment for gender dysphoria. In general, counselors must educate families on the detrimental effects of withholding medical interventions, including increased psychiatric comorbidity (e.g., suicidality, substance abuse). Alternatively, there are risks inherent in hormonal or surgical interventions, including the timing of administration and the irreversible nature of some of these interventions. Because the client is 13 years old, their ability to make an informed decision may not be developmentally appropriate, particularly for hormonal and surgical interventions. The principle of beneficence is honored by working for the good of the client's overall mental health and wellbeing. Fidelity is the ethical principle that is used when keeping commitments and promises. Fidelity is most commonly practiced when conducting research and engaging with other professionals.

10. D: The purpose of supporting the client's use of self-identified, gender-affirming pronouns is to normalize and validate gender diversity as a natural human variation. Some research has shown that gender-affirmative care is associated with improved outcomes for gender dysphoria. Counselors using gender-affirmative care provide a safe and supportive environment for gender-diverse individuals through advocacy, psychoeducation, and person-centered counseling. Social transitions for TGNC include identifying preferred pronouns; however, the counselor's primary purpose for using preferred pronouns in family therapy is to affirm, normalize, and validate gender diversity. Gender diversity is fluid; therefore, the client may or may not use the same pronouns in the future.

11. B: Structural family therapy's primary purpose is to strengthen the boundaries within family systems. Counselors accomplish this by deliberately disrupting the family's homeostasis through techniques that include unbalancing, blocking transactional patterns, and shifting boundaries. Additional structural family therapy techniques include assigning tasks, reframing, escalating stress, psychoeducation, and developing implicit conflict. Contextual family therapy emphasizes the ethical elements of each family, including loyalty, trust, and relational principles. Murray Bowen developed multigenerational (extended) family systems theory, which focuses on families with high levels of emotional fusion and low levels of differentiation. Bowenian therapists use multigenerational transmission process to assess how a family's dysfunctional interactions can be handed down from generation to generation. Strategic family therapy places much less emphasis on boundaries; instead, it focuses on patterns of communication and interactions. Some techniques of strategic family therapy include paradoxical intervention, pretend techniques, and hypothesizing.

12. C: Reframing is used to help the client reconceptualize the problem and allow them to shift their perspective. In this situation, a reframe would emphasize the father's commitment to counseling and his desire to understand as a possible indication of love and acceptance. Restructuring is used in family therapy when counselors intentionally unbalance the family's homeostasis to facilitate transformation and improve interactions and functioning. Linking is a group therapy technique employed by group leaders to help members connect with one another. Joining is a family systems technique that refers to the counselor taking a leadership position within the family system. In structural family therapy, joining also involves blending, tracking, and mimesis.

13. D: According to the DSM-5, gender dysphoria is associated with all of the answer choices except ADHD. Per the DSM-5, "Clinically referred adolescents with gender dysphoria appear to have comorbid mental disorders, with anxiety and depressive disorders being the most common. As in children, autism spectrum disorder is more prevalent in clinically referred adolescents with gender dysphoria than in the general population" (APA, 2013). For most males, adolescence starts between the ages of 10 and 14. Identifying comorbid diagnoses or symptoms can help counselors select appropriate interventions and address any additional barriers affecting the client. For example, considerations for gender-diverse individuals on the autism spectrum may require a tailored approach for effectively handling social transitions and interpersonal relationships.

Case Study 4

1. B: According to the DSM-5, Criterion B for the diagnosis of depressive disorder due to another medical condition (migraine headache) states that the diagnoses can be made if "there is evidence … that the disturbance is the direct pathophysiological consequence of another medical condition" (APA, 2013). When making this determination, "the clinician must consider the possibility that the mood symptoms are caused by the physiological consequences of the medical condition rather than the medication, in which case depressive disorder due to another medical condition is diagnosed … If the clinician has ascertained that the disturbance is a function of another medical condition and substance use or withdrawal, both diagnoses (i.e., depressive disorder due to another medical condition and substance/medication-induced depressive disorder) may be given" (APA, 2013). Lastly, psychological and cultural effects are considerations for all diagnoses and are not stipulated criteria for this diagnosis.

2. B: Research indicates that depression and migraine headaches may be reduced by engaging in progressive relaxation. Progressive relaxation involves tensing and releasing muscle groups one by one. Biofeedback training is a similar exercise in that muscle relaxation is involved; however, biofeedback uses an external monitoring device to measure physiological responses. Instruments provide information or feedback on specific measures under the participant's control (e.g., heart rate, body temperature, muscle tension). Autogenic training is used to promote relaxation by "telling" one's body to relax using verbal prompts (e.g., "your arms are becoming heavy"). Rhythmic breathing provides relaxation by inhaling and exhaling slowly (e.g., "count to five as you inhale and as you exhale").

3. A: The DAS measures a couple's levels of relationship distress and includes the following four subscales: (1) dyadic consensus (i.e., how well the couple agrees with one another), (2) dyadic satisfaction (i.e., how content the couple is with the relationship), (3) dyadic cohesion (i.e., how well the couple engages in activities with one another), and (4) affectual expression (i.e., agreed-upon emotional and affectional expression). The DAS, which consists of a 32-item self-rated assessment instrument, is used to measure levels of perceived distress for couples in committed relationships. The MMQ is also a self-assessment. The MMQ uses two subscales to measure relational and sexual connectedness. The PAIR inventory identifies five forms of intimacy for a couple: emotional, recreational, sexual, social, and intellectual. The MAQ measures secure, avoidant, and anxious-ambivalent attachment styles.

4. C: Summarizing shared concerns and assessing readiness for change can help create a therapeutic alliance with the couple. During the initial stage of treatment, building a therapeutic alliance can be accomplished by assisting the couple in conceptualizing the presenting problem. This can be done by using core counseling techniques, including, but not limited to, summarization, empathy, attending, encouraging, genuineness, and congruence. In addition, counselors can use a motivational enhancement approach to determine a couple's readiness for change. Assessing a couple's readiness to change contributes to the therapeutic alliance by fostering hope. Explaining your clinical approach to define the treatment focus is not the best option because it does not elicit the couple's input for what they need and hope to get out of therapy. Empathizing and validating the client's pain addresses the client's needs, but this does not address the couple's needs. Further, this response may alienate the husband and potentially deprive him of the opportunity to later express this sentiment to his wife. Encouraging "I" statements and problem solving are helpful interventions, but this is not the best option for creating a collaborative therapeutic alliance.

5. C: Eye movement desensitization and reprocessing treats childhood trauma by using bilateral stimulation to activate portions of the brain and release blocked emotional experiences. Eye movement desensitization and reprocessing is based on the adaptive information processing model and requires specialized training for use; it involves a sequence of steps used to remove distressing emotional blocks so healing can begin. Neuro-linguistic programming providers claim that there is a connection between neurological processes, language, and patterns of behavior that can be learned through experience or programming. Critics of the method suggest that the theory is supported by anecdotal evidence only (i.e., it is not an evidence-based practice). Acceptance and commitment therapy uses various techniques to help individuals accept (instead of fight) their present-moment thoughts and feelings so behavioral changes can occur. Finally, interpersonal psychotherapy is a time-limited intervention used to improve one's social functioning to decrease emotional distress. It addresses the components of a person's social isolation, grief, life transitions, and/or interpersonal disputes.

6. C: Created by Sue Johnson, emotionally focused couples therapy considers the influence of early childhood experiences on emotional connection and attachment. The impact of the client's experiences of neglect likely affects her emotional engagement and feelings of safety and security in the relationship. Counselors using emotionally focused couples therapy help decrease relational distress using steps found in the following three sequential stages: (1) de-escalation, which is used to help the couple see their pattern of negative interactions characterized by self-reinforcing cycles; (2) restructuring interactions—shaping new experiences for couples to connect and form emotional attachments with one another; and (3) consolidation and integration, which is the process used to help clients apply their newly shaped connections to their presenting problems. Person-centered and other humanistic therapies are a part of emotionally focused couples therapy; however, this is not a stand-alone treatment for attachment.

Cognitive-behavioral couples therapy is a short-term intervention that uses social learning theory and behavioral therapy concepts to help clients cognitively reconstruct beliefs that contribute to relationship distress. Although certain "core beliefs" may be grounded in a partner's childhood experiences, couples CBT does not exclusively examine attachment. Lastly, solution-focused therapy for couples is a short-term approach used to help assess a couple's strengths by inquiring about times when there are exceptions to the problem. Solution-focused therapy is not commonly used to examine early childhood experiences or the origins of attachment.

7. B: Parallel parenting is effective for divorced parents who have low degrees of cooperation and high degrees of conflict. Parallel parenting allows parents to disengage from one another but remain engaged in their children's lives. After disengagement, plans are made that determine who is responsible for various parenting domains, such as medical and educational care. Parents form independent relationships with teachers, doctors, and coaches, and communication between the parents is generally conducted via email or through a neutral third party. This approach would benefit the primary client because she would feel less of the burden in raising her husband's son, in addition to benefiting her husband and her husband's ex-wife, therefore relieving stress on the entire unit. Cooperative parenting works best with high-cooperation and low-conflict parents. Parents who engage in cooperative parenting effectively communicate with one another and agree on shared responsibilities. Collaborative parenting is used interchangeably with cooperative parenting, making it the preferred approach for couples who communicate effectively and engage in mutual decision making. Parents who use an authoritarian approach emphasize strict obedience and inflict harsh punishments when rules are broken. Using this approach as a form of "tough love" for the husband's child is ill advised and could be detrimental to the child's overall well-being.

8. C: Aaron Beck used the term cognitive triad to refer to negative beliefs one has about oneself, one's world, and one's future. Beck is known for the cognitive theory of depression. Albert Ellis founded REBT. William Glasser is associated with reality therapy, and Frederick Perls is known for gestalt therapy.

9. A: You are hoping to create new experiences of emotional attachment. Emotionally focused couples therapy uses enactments to counterbalance negative interactions, uncover underlying vulnerabilities, and develop emotional attunement. Enactments increase awareness of emotional attachment by encouraging couples to engage with one another directly. Counselors using emotionally focused couples therapy enactments first work to identify the couple's negative patterns of interaction. Counselors then help couples safely address vulnerabilities to create secure bonds with one another. Creating change talk by reducing ambivalence is a motivational interviewing technique. Although it is helpful to assess readiness for change with the couple, this is not accomplished by using enactments. Transference and countertransference are not present in this interaction. The technique of mirroring is used in imago couples therapy. Therapists use mirroring to encourage the message receiver to paraphrase or mirror back exactly what was conveyed by the message sender.

10. D: This is an example of validating. Imago relationship therapy, developed by Dr. Harville Hendrix and Dr. Helen LaKelly Hunt, uses imago dialogue, or an imago intentional dialogue, which is a technique used with couples to facilitate meaningful dialogue rather than unproductive discussions that fuel criticism, judgment, and contempt. There are three steps to an imago dialogue: (1) mirroring (i.e., "what I hear you say is ..."), in which the sender's message is reflected by using methods such as paraphrasing, summarizing, and clarification; (2) validating (i.e., "you make sense because ..."), which conveys to the sender that the receiver has accurately understood the message and conveys how it made sense to them; and (3) empathizing, (i.e., "I imagine this feels ..."), which involves processing the message sender's underlying feelings. Attending is a listening skill used throughout the process. Couples demonstrate attending using eye contact, facing their partner, and remaining focused.

11. C: The Columbia-Suicide Severity Rating Scale is a comprehensive suicide risk assessment appropriate for this client. It is used in multiple settings, including outpatient behavioral health, and it provides an in-depth assessment of suicidal ideation and suicidal behavior. The Patient Health Questionnaire-2 is a two-question abbreviated scale used to evaluate the frequency of depressed mood and anhedonia within the past 2 weeks. The Achenbach System of Empirically Based Assessment uses multiple informants to assess an individual's adaptive and maladaptive behaviors. The Ask Suicide-Screening Questions toolkit consists of four screening questions and is designed for individuals ages 10 to 24.

12. B: You are trying to determine the client's protective factors. Protective factors mitigate suicide risk and include coping skills, social support, religious beliefs, and restricted access to lethal means. The client's level of marital distress is a risk factor that has already been determined. Religious or spiritual support is one example of a protective factor; however, the question is posed to help determine all protective factors. This question is one of a series of questions posed as part of a suicide risk assessment, which helps guide recommendations for an appropriate level of care (e.g., outpatient, inpatient, residential).

13. C: The National Action Alliance for Suicide Prevention: Transforming Health Systems Initiative Work Group's *Recommended Standard Care for People with Suicide Risk: Making Health Care Suicide Safe* (2018) contains recommendations for treating suicidality. All of the elements (safety planning, means reduction, and caring contacts) except supervision are included in the recommended standard care. EBPs for outpatient behavioral health include conducting a safety plan intervention during sessions when the concern for suicide risk is high. Safety planning includes frequently assessing suicidal risk and updating the safety plan during each visit until the risk subsides. Means reduction involves assessing for lethal means and arranging for their removal or reduction. Caring contacts is another evidence-based standard and practice. Caring contacts are staff members or other individuals who provide brief support to clients during high-risk periods, such as transitioning from hospitalization to a lower level of care or for missed appointments. Contacts are made via phone, texts, or letters to help prevent isolation and reduce the risk for suicide.

Case Study 5

1. D: Repeated nightmares involving being away from home are criteria for separation anxiety disorder. Separation anxiety disorder is characterized by excessive fear of either being apart from or losing an attachment figure (e.g., away from home). Persistent and excessive fear of teachers and peers is better explained by a specific phobia, whereas hypervigilance, poor concentration, and sleep disturbance may indicate a generalized anxiety disorder. Selective mutism is a form of anxiety in children associated with the failure to speak in social situations where there is the expectation that a child would do so.

2. D: The DSM-5 criteria for GAD includes excessive anxiety and worry (chronic apprehensive expectation). When the clinical presentation includes an acute stressor, the distress may be better explained by diagnoses such as post-traumatic stress disorder or acute stress disorder. Separation anxiety is considered when the distress is explained by separation from attachment figures. Lastly, obsessive-compulsive disorder is characterized by intrusive and unwanted thoughts or images.

3. D: Hypothesized psychological vulnerabilities for GAD include cognitive biases. Counselors assess clients for vulnerabilities to help identify specific factors that may predispose someone to certain psychological disorders. Psychological vulnerabilities for GAD include cognitive biases, insecure attachment, unstable affect management, and unconscious conflicts. Biological vulnerabilities include sleep irregularities and autonomic hyperactivity, which is a physiological component of GAD and includes physiological symptoms such as dry mouth, heart palpitations, and sweating. Negative rather than positive valence systems are associated with GAD. Negative valence includes affective states such as anxiety and depression, whereas positive valence includes happiness and joy. Social vulnerabilities, such as trauma, certain parenting styles, and peer rejection, are also associated with GAD development.

4. B: Disqualifying or discounting the positive is a cognitive distortion associated with the client's worry. Disqualifying the positive is the belief that one's accomplishments don't count. For example, the client is the number-one ranked player on her high school varsity tennis team, yet she is dissatisfied with her less-than-perfect performance on the tennis court. Mind reading is a cognitive distortion that happens when one claims, without evidence, that other people's reactions to them are negative. Emotional reasoning is also a cognitive distortion; it occurs when one engages in self-judgment based on emotional reactions. It is the belief that negative emotions define an individual as a person (e.g., "I'm experiencing anxiety; therefore, I am in danger"). Black-and-white, or all-or-nothing, thinking happens when there is no acknowledgment of any "shades of gray" (e.g., "Either I fail or I succeed").

5. B: Integrating contextualized factors in treatment interventions is the best way to enhance the family's motivation and adherence to treatment. Integrating contextual factors is one method that counselors use to help establish a therapeutic alliance, enhance motivation, and increase treatment adherence. Examples of contextualized elements include race, ethnicity, gender, spirituality, and culture. The client is an African American female with concerns about fitting in with her predominantly white peers. When delivering contextualized treatment interventions, the client's and counselor's racial and ethnic identity and positionality (i.e., privileged versus marginalized) must also be considered. Offering a selection of treatment modalities during the initial stages of therapy may not be appropriate or desired. Coordinating treatment with youth-serving systems is vital to the client's care but is not the best way to influence motivation and treatment adherence. Counselors provide written verbal explanations of informed consent and transparent back-and-forth discussions to help foster a clear understanding of all components of informed consent before obtaining an agreement.

6. A: The GAD-7 is an anxiety rating scale that includes an instrument for use with adolescents and a version that allows a parent to fill out scales on their child. The GAD-7 is a seven-item self-administered instrument used to identify some of the criteria for general anxiety disorder and to determine symptom severity. The CPRS-HI is a questionnaire that asks parents about symptoms related to attention-deficit hyperactivity disorder. There is also a version for teachers. The HAM-A is a 14-item scale that measures the severity of anxiety symptoms. It does not have a version for parents to complete on their child. The PHQ-9: Parent Report is used to measure depression rather than anxiety.

7. C: You and your supervisor appropriately determine that you must respect the client's privacy unless she permits you to view her social media account. The ACA Code of Ethics addresses this issue in Section H.6.c, entitled "Client Virtual Presence." In this scenario, you searched for the client's social media account without prior permission. You appropriately discuss the ethical dilemma with your supervisor. Per the ACA Code of Ethics, counselors "are expected to engage in a carefully considered ethical decision-making process." This process generally involves determining the scope of the problem, applying the code of ethics, consulting supervisors and other appropriate professionals, and determining the best course of action. You not only viewed a private account without permission but did not have grounds for suspicion. The client stated that she felt like she didn't fit in with her peers and equated her number of likes with her worth as a person; this did not include allegations of cyberbullying or other safety-related concerns.

8. B: Dependency and inclusion describe the preaffiliation, or forming, stage of group development. This initial phase of group development is marked by apprehension and tentative exploration. The group leader's involvement is most pronounced during this stage. Healthy time-limited or closed groups have distinct beginning, middle, and end stages (i.e., forming, storming, norming, performing, and adjourning). Power and control describe the middle stage of group development. Other descriptors for this stage include storming, counterdependency, and flight. Competition and the struggle for control emerge as the authority of the group leader is challenged during this stage. Structure and trust describe the norming stage, which transpires during the working stage of development. The leader's role is less pronounced during this stage, and the group members form closer connections. Separation, or adjourning, is associated with the last stage of group development.

9. C: Group leaders demonstrate the skill of executive functioning when establishing rules, setting limits, and developing a group-specific termination (i.e., discharge) plan. In other words, the group leader must remain vigilant of the group dynamics and set boundaries appropriately. Members are clear on the number of sessions held, and counselors establish the minimal discharge criteria. Lieberman et al. (1973) identified core group leadership functions as executive functioning, caring, emotional stimulation, and meaning attribution. Fostering autonomy and differentiation are therapeutic considerations for the middle stage of group development. Leaders execute meaning attribution when promoting insight and understanding among group members. Group leaders exhibit emotional stimulation at varying intervals by assessing emotional exchanges and stimulating or controlling levels of emotional expression.

10. A: The likely source of these feelings is countertransference. Countertransference occurs when the therapist emotionally reacts to transference happening among group members. Countertransference can either be subjective (i.e., stemming from unresolved past issues) or objective (i.e., stemming from the difficult personalities of group members). Transference involves the unconscious transfer of feelings and reactions to another person or experience encountered in the present moment. Transference occurs in individual and group therapy. When transference happens in group therapy, it can happen with the group leader or other group members. The group is not exhibiting unhealthy dynamics because they are in the middle, or storming, stage of group development, characterized by struggles for power and control. Lastly, because countertransference is a normal experience, it is not caused by underdeveloped leadership skills. However, therapists must be attuned to the present-moment experience required for understanding the subgroup's behavior.

11. C: Acceptance of all group members would most likely indicate that the group has successfully moved to the next stage of development. The group is currently in the middle, or storming, stage of group development. The storming stage is characterized by conflict among members, challenges toward group leaders, and the formation of alliances or subgroups. During this phase, members vie for leadership roles as the desire for power and control becomes more pronounced. According to Tuckman (1984), there are five phases of group development: (1) the forming stage is marked by avoidance of controversy, apprehension, and tentative exploration, (2) the aforementioned storming phase, (3) the norming stage, in which structure and trust evolve and all members are accepted as the group begins to bond together, (4) the performing stage, in which the group functions as a unit working toward common goals, and (5) the final stage, adjourning, in which the group's momentum slows as the group prepares to separate and say goodbye.

12. A: The best response to the negative interaction is to block the negative behavior and reestablish protective norms. It is important to note that the group is in the storming stage of development. Without group cohesion, the group leader must keep members safe by taking charge and addressing conflict. Reestablishing group norms and rules involves reminders about the group rules, tasks, and purpose. Universality, one of Irvin Yalom's group therapeutic factors, helps clients feel less alone as they relate to one another's experiences. This is not achieved by placing pressure on the client to share, particularly as it may relate to experiences of shame. Linking connects group members to foster universality. Groups need to have a here-and-now focus, which would not apply to feelings that the client experienced in the past. Imparting information, also one of Yalom's therapeutic factors, is not necessarily accomplished by offering your interpretation of the interaction. In doing so, you may risk isolating the client, the subgroup, and other group members.

13. D: You attend to all of the key elements listed except identifying members in need of a booster session. According to the American Group Psychotherapy Association (AGPA) Practice Guidelines for Group Psychotherapy (AGPA, n.d.), factors listed in answer options A, B, and C summarize the responsibilities of group leaders during the final phase of group therapy. Empirical evidence shows that scheduling booster sessions for all group members helps prevent symptom relapse. Identifying candidates in need of a booster session is rarely processed with the group as a whole.

Case Study 6

1. D: The MMSE includes the question "What are the three objects that I asked you to remember a few moments ago?" The MMSE is one method used to quantify an individual's cognitive functioning. In addition to recall, the MMSE assesses orientation, language, mathematical calculation, attention, and motor skills. The CSDD is a screening tool used to help detect symptoms of depression in individuals experiencing dementia. The CSDD measures a broad range of symptoms, including mood, behavioral disturbances, eating, sleeping, and suicidality. The Vineland-II is an assessment tool rather than a screening instrument. The Vineland-II measures several factors, including daily functioning, adaptive functioning, emotional disturbance, and other behavioral health conditions. Finally, the DLA-20 is an assessment instrument measuring multiple domains, including time management, safety, and communication. The DLA-20 is useful for establishing baseline measures and can be used again at various treatment intervals to measure outcomes.

2. C: According to the DSM-5's description of mild neurocognitive disorder, "The cognitive deficits do not interfere with capacity for independence in everyday activities (i.e., complex instrumental activities of daily living such as paying bills or managing medications are preserved, but greater effort, compensatory strategies, or accommodation may be required)" (APA, 2013). It is not true that these deficits must occur exclusively in the context of a delirium, nor are deficits so severe that they disrupt activities of daily living or instrumental activities of daily living.

3. D: Difficulty remembering names of acquaintances is not a symptom or observation included in the social cognition domain. In the DSM-5, Criteria A, the diagnosis of mild neurocognitive disorder (MND) is confirmed when there is "evidence of modest cognitive decline from a previous level of performance in one or more cognitive domains (complex attention, executive function, learning, and memory, language, perceptual-motor, or social cognition)" (APA, 2013). Symptoms or observations of individuals who "avoid use of specific names of acquaintances" (APA, 2013) is included in the language domain. Further, the DSM-5 defines the cognitive domains associated with neurocognitive disorders which also includes "examples of symptoms or observations regarding impairments in everyday activities, and examples of assessments" (APA, 2013).

4. B: A person-centered approach is reflected in the statement "Your heart is heavy after leaving a career that was once everything to you." Person-centered therapists facilitate unconditional positive regard, empathy, and genuineness. The aforementioned statement is an expression of empathy. The statement "You have a deep conviction that some of your best years were before retirement," is an example of a cognitive-behavioral approach, with the client's thoughts expressed as deep convictions. Psychoanalytic therapy is reflected in the statement "Your sadness and the person you are today are likely the results of unconscious processes." Person-centered therapists focus on the conscious rather than the unconscious. Finally, the statement, "You're grieving a heavy loss. How does that affect your present-day, here-and-now experiences?" characterizes gestalt therapy.

5. A: Despite never working with a client diagnosed with MND, your education, experience, and training should provide you with the skills to treat the client's anxiety, apathy, and depression. You can provide supportive counseling, address psychosocial symptoms, teach coping skills, and suggest compensatory memory strategies. Section C.2 of the ACA Code of Ethics states that counselors must only practice within the boundaries of their competence, which is specifically based on "their education, training, supervised experience, state and national professional credentials, and appropriate professional experience." Counselors have an ongoing ethical responsibility to remain current and increase their knowledge base by obtaining continuing education, but this would not be a prerequisite for working with this client. The counselor would not necessarily need the PET scan results to proceed because a mental status exam and neuropsychological report both show MND and associated behavioral disturbances.

6. B: The client scored one standard deviation below the mean. This signifies that she scored as well as or better than 16% of the population because the percentage of the normed population that scores plus or minus one standard deviation is 68% and the percentage that scores greater than one standard deviation is an additional 16%. In that case, an individual who scores less than one standard deviation of the mean would be scoring as well as or better than the remaining 16% who scored more than one standard deviation less than the mean. The normal curve is symmetrically distributed. Almost two-thirds of the scores lie one standard deviation from the mean. Roughly 3% of the population tested scored two standard deviations below the mean. Generally, standardized tests have a mean score of 100. With a mean of 100, one standard deviation below the mean would be a score of 85 rather than 85% (whereas one standard deviation above the mean would be a score of 115). If the client scored at least two standard deviations below the mean, she would likely receive the diagnosis of major neurocognitive disorder.

7. B: Summarizing the client's key concerns and identified areas of focus would best engage the client and her daughter. The daughter is not the client; however, she presents today as a collateral contact and an individual who may impact engaging the client in treatment. Summarizing is a communication skill used to tie together various issues and feelings expressed by the client. This is helpful because it narrows the client's identified areas of focus, helps the client feel heard, and allows the counselor to ask for corrections and clarifications. Individuals with MND have cognitive difficulties beyond the normal aging process, making answer A incorrect. Although constructing a genogram provides valuable information on the family, it is not the best way to engage the client in treatment. Giving advice does not contribute to engagement and should be reserved for safety issues and should be used sparingly, if at all, during treatment. Catastrophizing and negative predictions are cognitive distortions and irrational beliefs found in rational-emotional therapy and cognitive therapy, respectively.

8. B: Reminiscence therapy uses tangible memory triggers (e.g., photographs, music, household items) to prompt discussions of past experiences. Reminiscence therapy, validation therapy, cognitive stimulation therapy, and reality orientation are evidence-based psychosocial interventions for persons experiencing cognitive impairment. Reminiscence therapy improves factors associated with an individual's quality of life, such as depression and apathy. Validation therapy is based on the premise that individuals with cognitive impairment present with confusion to escape reality and do so to avoid loneliness, isolation, and distress. Validation therapy recognizes, respects, and values each individual's qualities and feelings rather than focusing on their experiences of confusion. Cognitive stimulation therapy typically consists of a variety of activities, puzzles, and games used to improve one's memory. Cognitive stimulation therapy may also include elements of reality orientation. Reality orientation works by increasing an individual's awareness of time, location, and surroundings. This is typically done by placing this information on a dry-erase board in an individual's home or residence.

9. C: The primary purpose of asking the client to share her experiences of attending church, going to her book club, and taking fitness classes is to underscore the value of renewing and maintaining social support and exercise. The client is experiencing a decline in cognitive functioning but also exhibits associated behavioral and emotional disturbances. Supportive social relationships and exercise are associated with an overall increase in one's quality of life and decreased experiences of depression and anxiety. It is unnecessary to determine the client's cognitive functioning before discontinuing activities because we already have evidence of a modest cognitive decline from a previous level of functioning. Because the client is adhering to treatment thus far, individualized belief systems do not need to be examined. Lastly, cognitive impairments rather than interpersonal stressors or trauma are linked to the client's discontinuation of the activities.

10. D: Empathetic reflecting or empathetic responding is used when a counselor responds to the client's verbal expressions and underlying emotions. Paraphrasing is used when a counselor responds to the client's main idea or literal meaning without using the client's exact words. Counselors use attending by demonstrating listening and paying attention to the client. This occurs when making eye contact or assuming an attentive posture. Reframing is a communication skill that counselors use to help clients view things from a different and more positive perspective.

11. B: The 2014 ACA Code of Ethics (Standard A.6.a) addresses multiple relationships stating, "Counselors consider the risks and benefits of accepting as clients those with whom they have had a previous relationship. ... When counselors accept these clients, they take appropriate professional precautions such as informed consent, consultation, supervision, and documentation to ensure that judgment is not impaired and no exploitation occurs" (ACA, 2014). Signed waivers granting permission for the counselor to proceed with the client, despite the risk involved, are not included in the professional precautions that counselors must take.

12. C: In terms of the supervisor's and counselor's ethical guidelines for collecting outstanding copays, standard A.10.d of the ACA Code of Ethics states, "If counselors intend to use collection agencies or take legal measures to collect fees from clients who do not pay for services as agreed upon, they include such information in their informed consent documents and also inform clients in a timely fashion of intended actions and offer clients the opportunity to make payment." *Pro bono publico* refers to providing services with little or no financial return. Applying this concept to eliminating a client's copay after billing insurance is prohibited when billing the Centers for Medicare & Medicaid Services and is ethically risky otherwise. Fee splitting is listed as an unacceptable business practice in sanction A.10.b of the ACA Code of Ethics. Lastly, verbal agreements about the copays being written off may be a consideration, but this is not the best reflection of the supervisor's or counselor's ethical responsibility.

13. B: The best choice for this client is to refer her to another professional who can address her memory impairment. Because the client's PET scan identified changes associated with Alzheimer's disease, you would need to find a specialist, such as a neuropsychologist, who could better address the client's cognitive impairment. Discussing termination is a possibility, but it precludes the client benefiting from additional resources. Continuing to work with the client on improving her memory impairment is also a possibility. However, research shows cognitive impairment is progressive, and there is little more the counselor can do to help with this. Renewing client treatment goals for depression and apathy is unnecessary because the client has already achieved them. This would only apply if the client met her short-term goals and the counselor and client decide together to focus on long-term goals.

Case Study 7

1. C: BPD is clustered with similar personality disorders characterized by dramatic and overly emotional behavior. The DSM-5 groups personality disorders into three clusters (i.e., cluster A, cluster B, and cluster C). Cluster A includes paranoid, schizoid, and schizotypal personality disorders. Individuals with personality disorders in cluster A often exhibit odd or eccentric behavior. Cluster B personality disorders include borderline, histrionic, antisocial, and narcissistic personality disorders. Individuals with cluster B personality disorders can be described as dramatic, emotional, or erratic. Cluster C includes avoidant, dependent, and obsessive-compulsive personality disorders. Individuals in cluster C are characterized as anxious and fearful.

2. D: The client does not experience grandiosity as a symptom indicative of BPD. Grandiosity is a symptom of narcissistic personality disorder. BPD is characterized by fear of real or imagined abandonment, suicidality, and intensive anger. According to the DSM-5, BPD is characterized by "a pervasive pattern of instability of interpersonal relationships, self-image, and affects, and [by] marked impulsivity" (APA, 2013). Recurrent suicidal behavior is a criterion that is separate from "frantic efforts to avoid real or imagined abandonment" (APA, 2013) and impulsivity. The client's fear of abandonment manifests in her romantic and interpersonal relationships. Although suicidal behavior is a separate criterion, worries about separation or abandonment can contribute to acts of suicide or self-harm.

3. A: Individuals subject to confirmation bias seek information that confirms an initial hypothesis while rejecting information that does not fit the theory. An unstructured interview consists of open-ended questions used to arrive at a diagnosis, whereas structured interviews use a standardized list of questions. Semistructured assessments offer flexibility between the two. Unstructured interviews are subject to bias, particularly for an unseasoned clinician. Overconfidence bias, a form of hindsight bias, occurs when counselors overestimate their ability to make sound clinical decisions. Overconfidence bias occurs when answers to difficult clinical decisions seem apparent when viewed retrospectively. Affect heuristic is used when counselors base clinical decisions on the feelings experienced when interacting with a client. For example, if a client becomes angry or irrational during a diagnostic assessment, which produces countertransference, the counselor may be quick to assign a BPD diagnosis. The Hawthorne effect is the tendency for individuals to change their behavior in response to knowing they are being monitored or observed.

4. A: Carl Jung would most likely view the combination of the client's attire and her recent suicide attempt stemming from a bad breakup as her persona. Jung described the persona as "the social face the individual presented to the world—a kind of mask, designed on the one hand to make a definite impression upon others, and on the other to conceal the true nature of the individual" (Jung, 1953). The client's sexualized manner of dress may serve as a means of concealing the true nature of her pain and underlying fear of abandonment. Jung is also known for the Electra complex, which he used to describe a female's unconscious desire for her father's love and attention. The anima, another concept originating from Jung, refers to the unconscious feminine side of a man. Finally, parapraxis is a Freudian concept used to describe an unconscious slip of the tongue or Freudian slip.

5. C: The desire to cause harm, feel better, or end distressing feelings permanently is more indicative of suicidal self-injury than NSSI. Suicidality differs from NSSI in that there is a desire to permanently end feelings. In contrast, with NSSI, there is a chronic or persistent urge to cause harm to oneself to regulate or detach from distressing emotions. The DSM-5 has proposed criteria for further research concerning NSSI. Criterion includes 5 or more days per year of deliberately engaging in self-harm. With NSSI, there is no suicidal intent. Instead, there is the expectation that the self-inflicted damage relieves a negative feeling or cognitive state. NSSI may also include intentional injury associated with feeling distressed, anxious, sad, or tense. Feelings immediately before the act may also be coupled with self-criticism. Finally, NSSI is associated with the persistent urge to cause harm that is often difficult to resist.

6. D: The TAPS tool has a screening component followed by a short assessment. The first component (TAP-1) screens for tobacco, alcohol, prescription medication, and other substance use. If the individual has a positive screen, it can be followed by a brief substance-specific assessment (TAPS-2). The CRAFFT screening test is used with adolescents aged 12-21 to screen for risk factors associated with substance use. The CAGE is a brief (i.e., four-question) screening instrument for alcohol use. Finally, the MAST is a screening instrument used to determine symptoms of alcohol dependency.

7. A: You engage in contract setting to help establish trust and build a working alliance. When you work with the client to establish trust and a collaborative working alliance, there is an increased likelihood of the client engaging in and benefiting from therapy. Although contract setting is helpful for addressing other issues, answer A is the best response. Eliminating client splitting and eliminating manipulation are not collaborative goals, making answer option B incorrect. Client contracts do not provide legal protection in the event of a boundary violation. It is the counselor's responsibility rather than the client's to ensure that boundaries are clearly defined and kept intact. Lastly, using contracts to give grounds for termination is not the primary purpose of contract setting.

8. C: The ethical principle that would best guide your response to the client's request to exclude safety issues from her treatment plan is autonomy. The ACA Code of Ethics includes ethical principles fundamental to ethical decision making. Autonomy is defined as "fostering the right to control the direction of one's life" (ACA, 2014). In this situation, it is appropriate to consider the client's autonomy by deciding which items go on her treatment plan. Clients have a right to accept or deny treatment. This does not mean that you do not assess and document the client's safety issues each session. It would be unethical not to assess the client's safety and provide safety-related interventions as needed. This topic can also be revisited in future sessions after trust has been established. Veracity is an ethical principle that calls for counselors to be truthful in their professional communication. Justice is honored when counselors stand up for equality and promote equity. Lastly, beneficence is achieved when counselors work for the well-being of clients and society at large.

9. B: Schema-focused therapy is an EBP for BPD. It uses a process known as limited reparenting to help clients establish a secure attachment with counselors within the confines of their professional relationship. The goal of schema-focused therapy is to help the client replace maladaptive schemas or negative patterns of behaving, thinking, and feeling with healthier experiences and interactions. Transference-focused psychotherapy is also an EBP for BPD. Transference-focused psychotherapy is a psychoanalytic therapy based, in part, on the assumption that primary defense mechanisms (e.g., "splitting" and "all-or-nothing" thinking) stem from identity defusion that fuels intense emotional states, transference, and strained interpersonal relationships. Dialectical behavior therapy, another EBP for BPD, is a combination of cognitive therapy, behavioral shaping, and mindfulness practices to overcome erratic patterns of emotions and behaviors. Lastly, mentalization-based treatment is an EBP that uses a psychodynamic approach to examine one's capacity to understand oneself in relation to others. The counselor identifies and addresses certain mental states that contribute to impulsivity and unstable interpersonal relationships.

10. D: The purpose of this activity is to encourage the client to take a nonjudgmental stance. You are using a component of dialectical behavior therapy, which is an empirically validated approach for BPD. This approach targets black-and-white or all-or-nothing dialects that characterize common thinking patterns among individuals with BPD. Mindfulness-based exercises are used to help the client stay fully aware of the present (i.e., here-and-now) moment. In this state of awareness, clients learn to accept and regulate intense emotions in a nonjudgmental fashion. Identifying core beliefs, teaching conflict resolution skills, and exploring transference and countertransference are also interventions for BPD; however, a nonjudgmental stance allows the client to have experiences that are "both-and" rather than "either-or."

11. A: Validation refers to a counselor's ability to provide acceptance while simultaneously facilitating change. Engaging in this paradox exemplifies a dialectical stance, which is to hold two seemingly opposed truths. It is a practice of dialectical behavior therapy that can help decrease the client's physiological and psychological arousal. In general, affirmations are statements acknowledging an individual's positive qualities or capabilities. Counselors use confirmation when establishing truth or certainty. Clarification is used when counselors seek understanding when ideas are expressed when statements are contradictory or difficult to understand.

12. C: Affect regulation consists of affect labeling, recognition of escalation points, mood monitoring, and cue identification. Affect labeling helps clients experience gradations of feeling by identifying and differentiating overwhelming emotions. Because individuals with BPD experience black-and-white thinking, there is a tendency to label feelings using polarized terms (e.g., "I'm either angry or calm"). Helping clients identify and articulate gradations of feeling (e.g., irritated, relieved) allows for the acknowledgment of shades of gray and eventually the client learning to tolerate a range of emotions. Recognition of escalation points breaks down the client's thinking, acting, and behaving before an unregulated emotional event. Mood monitoring is used to help clients keep track of patterns and changes in moods. Finally, cue identification helps identify problematic behaviors that can be altered. This is done by having the client identify internal cues rather than external triggers.

13. A: Gestalt therapists would identify the client's boundary disturbances as a way of responding to the client's resistance to change. Gestalt therapists use the term boundary disturbance to describe various forms of resistance. Boundary disturbances include projection, introjection, retroflection, confluence, and deflection. Gestalt therapists embrace the idea that individuals are the sum total of their mind, body, and soul. Integration of all components is the overall goal of gestalt therapy. Forceful disputing is a rational emotive behavior therapy (REBT) technique. Transactional analysis analyzes a client's life scripts, which are unconscious justifications for erroneous beliefs originating in childhood. Roll with resistance or rolling with resistance is used in motivational interviewing as a nonconfrontational means to help the client, rather than the counselor, argue for change.

Case Study 8

1. C: Fear of being trapped in situations in which escape is perceived as unlikely is a DSM-5 criterion for agoraphobia. Separation anxiety disorder is characterized by separation from an attachment figure. The fear of being judged in a social situation is associated with social anxiety disorder. Hoarding disorder involves the fear of parting with possessions despite excessive acquisition or clutter.

2. A: The DSM-5 lists negative events in childhood (e.g., the separation or death of a parent) as an environmental risk and prognostic factor for agoraphobia. Serious social neglect is associated with disinhibited social engagement disorder. Interpersonal physical and sexual abuse are environmental risk and prognostic factors for dissociative identity disorder. Lastly, neglect or lack of supervision is a risk and prognostic factor for pica.

3. B: A humanistic style uses a holistic approach to address a client's biopsychosocial and spiritual dimensions. Humanistic theories include person-centered therapy, gestalt therapy, and existential therapy. CBT's primary focus is to help clients change thought patterns characterized by erroneous, irrational, or negative beliefs. There are several examples of CBT, including REBT, dialectic behavior therapy, and cognitive therapy. Psychoanalytic theory addresses the effects of early childhood experiences on the unconscious mind. Behavioral therapy is based on the assumption that a person's behaviors can be changed through rewards, punishments, reinforcement, and desensitization.

4. D: Of the stages listed, contemplation is the one that is least likely to produce change. Prochaska and DiClemente's (1992) transtheoretical model of change consists of the following linear stages: precontemplation, contemplation, preparation, action, and maintenance. Individuals in stage 1, or the precontemplation stage, lack awareness of behaviors that may require change. In stage 2, the contemplation stage, individuals are aware that changes need to be made but are ambivalent about taking action. In stage 3, the preparation/determination stage, individuals acknowledge the detrimental consequences of their behavior and get ready to make a change. The action stage, or stage 4, is also known as the willpower stage because the person acknowledges that a change needs to be made and is taking steps to change. Finally, in stage 5, the maintenance stage, individuals take the action steps required to sustain change. Termination or relapse may follow the maintenance stage if changes are not necessary or sustained.

5. A: Insurance providers require clinicians to establish medical necessity when determining a client's appropriate level of care. Services must be medically necessary to receive provider reimbursement, including approval for the frequency, length, and duration of clinical services. Medical necessity determines preapproval and ongoing approval for authorized services. Medical necessity, service utilization, and functional impairment are considered when assigning a client's level of care. The level of care is used when determining the least restrictive setting for a client's treatment, with lower levels of care assigned to those receiving outpatient services and a higher level of care required for more restrictive settings (e.g., hospitalization to residential treatment). Diagnosis is a level-of-care consideration, but the diagnosis alone does not reflect functional impairment and the client's level of distress. In general, treatment summaries are insufficient for determining the level of care. A payor source refers to an individual or entity responsible for charges generated from treatment services. Payor sources request level of care assessments; they do not provide clinical assessment.

6. D: The client's family boundaries can be described as diffuse. Structural family therapists focus on boundaries among family members. Boundaries are rules or barriers within a family system that dictate the amount of contact that members have with each other and the larger community. Families with diffuse boundaries are also described as enmeshed, which is observed in families who have become overly dependent on one another. Flexible boundaries occur when the boundaries are neither too closed and isolated nor too open and rigid. Flexible boundaries and clear boundaries are synonymous. Structural family therapists view healthy boundaries as those with the flexibility to adapt to stressors, communicate, and adjust limits when needed. Disengaged boundaries are rigid, and family members are isolated from one another.

7. B: Walking up and down the stairs and repeating the exposure until the SUD rating drops by half is the most effective exposure exercise. For exposure exercises to work, the client must experience increased levels of anxiety. The client's ability to tolerate increased anxiety levels through prolonged exposure creates new neuropathways in the brain. This new neuropathway leads to the downregulation of the amygdala, which is responsible for the brain's flight-or-fight response. Using relaxation strategies, using a safe person during the exposure, and having an escape plan by carrying medication are all contraindicated because they do not allow the client to experience the increased anxiety that is required for exposure therapy.

8. B: An interoceptive exposure exercise that matches the client's needs would be to have the client spin around in a swivel chair to induce dizziness. Interoceptive exposure exercises help recreate internal sensations associated with panic attacks. One of the client's internal triggers is dizziness. Individuals with agoraphobia respond to somatic stimuli (e.g., dizziness) by avoiding situations or engaging in safety behaviors. Individuals must stay with internal sensations during the exposure until they dissipate or reach a lower, predetermined SUD rating. Exposure exercises can be interoceptive, in vivo, imaginal, or experienced through virtual reality.

9. D: The framework for CART assumes that low levels of carbon dioxide resulting from symptoms of anxiety and panic can be altered with shallow breathing and a cognitive sense of being in control. The CART approach measures $PaCO_2$ and respiration rates believed to be the primary or secondary causes of anxiety and panic. Individuals are instructed to breathe in ways that prevent hyperventilation. This is achieved by taking slow, shallow breaths. CART is based on the theory that deep breaths, such as those used in relaxation training, can induce hyperventilation, leading to increased fear and panic. Progressive relaxation, thermal biofeedback, and mindfulness meditation are also effective in reducing anxiety but do not attribute therapeutic change to increased levels of $PaCO_2$.

10. D: You should encourage her to follow up with the prescribing doctor. According to the ACA Code of Ethics, "Counselors practice only within the boundaries of their competence, based on their education, training, supervised experience, state and national professional credentials, and appropriate professional experience." Counselors do not have the competence required to help clients discontinue medication. Medical supervision may be required for clients taking benzodiazepines, particularly those taking higher doses for more extended periods. Obtaining a signed release to speak with her doctor is appropriate; however, requesting a tapering schedule to present to the client is not. The agency's psychiatrist is not the prescribing doctor, making answer B incorrect. Offering advice on how the client can gradually taper off the medication places the client at increased risk.

11. C: Interjurisdictional practice is not a part of informed consent for distance counseling or telehealth. Informed consent involves sharing clear and sufficient information with the client to make an informed decision about treatment participation. Interjurisdictional practice occurs when a counselor provides services to a client across state lines. This is a legal issue that counselors must rectify before providing distance counseling. Although temporary permission for interjurisdictional practice may exist, it is rare and far less likely to be included in informed consent. All other answer items can be found in Section H.2 of the ACA Code of Ethics, which outlines guidelines for informed consent and disclosure.

12. B: Counselors adhering to the ACA Code of Ethics "take reasonable precautions to ensure the confidentiality of information transmitted through any electronic means." Section H.3 states that counselors should take steps to verify the identity of the client, rather than their own identity and the client's identity. This should occur "at the beginning and throughout the therapeutic process." Section H.2.b states that "Counselors acknowledge the limitations of maintaining the confidentiality of electronic records and transmissions. They inform clients that individuals might have authorized or unauthorized access to such records or transmissions (e.g., colleagues, supervisors, employees, information technologists)." Finally, Section H.4.f states, "Counselors consider the differences between face-to-face and electronic communication (nonverbal and verbal cues) and how these may affect the counseling process. Counselors educate clients on how to prevent and address potential misunderstandings arising from the lack of visual cues and voice intonations when communicating electronically."

13. C: In addition to randomization, an intention-to-treat analysis best ensures that a study's conclusions are free from bias. An intention-to-treat analysis uses conclusions based on keeping all subjects in the treatment group they were randomized to, independent of what occurs later in the experiment. In other words, for randomized clinical trials, if half of the subjects dropped out of the study or conditions changed that affected their participation, they were still counted despite deviation from the protocol. A per-protocol analysis is the opposite of an intention-to-treat analysis. A per-protocol analysis excludes subjects who deviated from the protocol. If conducted alone, this analysis is subject to attrition bias. Transactional analysis is a psychoanalytic counseling theory used to analyze social transactions to determine one's ego state. Unlike intention-to-treat analysis, on-treatment analysis only includes data on subjects who received the treatment they were randomized to—those who deviated from the protocol were not counted.

Case Study 9

1. B: The DSM-5 classifies ADHD as a neurodevelopmental disorder. A separate DSM-5 classification is entitled "Disruptive, Impulse-Control, and Conduct Disorders." This classification includes oppositional defiant disorder, intermittent explosive disorder, conduct disorder, antisocial personality disorder, pyromania, and kleptomania. In addition, The DSM-5 classifies disinhibited social engagement disorder as a trauma- and stressor-related disorder.

2. A: According to the DSM-5, "In the general population, oppositional defiant disorder co-occurs with ADHD in approximately half of children with the combined presentation and about a quarter with the predominantly inattentive presentation. ... Anxiety disorders and major depressive disorder occur in a minority of individuals with ADHD but more often than in the general population. Intermittent explosive disorder occurs in a minority of adults with ADHD, but at rates above population levels" (APA, 2013).

3. C: Cost-effectiveness and duration of treatment are not components of EBP. Instead, EBP includes three factors: (1) the clinician's knowledge, skills, and expertise; (2) the client's culture, preferences, and values; and (3) research evidence with the least probability of bias (i.e., the best available research evidence). Experts including Norcross and Wampold (2011) have advocated for incorporating the therapeutic relationship into the definition of EBP.

4. C: At age 7, the client thinks concretely and begins to perform logical operations. Piaget's concrete operational stage of development occurs between the ages of 7 and 11. During this stage, children form mental operations or rules as evidenced by understanding concepts of conservation and reversibility. Piaget's next stage of development (occurring at ages of 12+), is the formal operational stage, in which children and adults can use deductive reasoning and logic and think abstractly. Individuals in the formal operational stage of development also have the ability to think about what-if, or hypothetical, situations.

5. C: Randomized control or clinical trials (RCTs) are associated with the highest level of evidence. The highest level of evidence (i.e., strength) refers to methodologies that are less likely to have biases or confounds. However, experts caution clinicians from using RCTs as the sole determination for EBP because application to clinical practice must also be considered. Correlational research designs, which are less rigorous than RCTs, determine if there is a relationship between two factors. Experimenters conducting quasiexperimental studies manipulate the independent variable but do not randomly assign subjects to a control group or an experimental group. Ex post facto (i.e., "after the fact") designs are quasiexperimental designs involving subjects who are not randomly assigned to groups. Additionally, the experimenter cannot manipulate the independent variable because it was a condition present before the study was conducted.

6. B: The CRS has rating scales for parents and teachers. The CRS can be used with children ages 6–18, and it assesses ADHD and associated comorbid disorders. Parent and teacher scales are critical for diagnostic purposes because ADHD must occur in more than one setting (e.g., at home and at school). The ADHD-RS-IV with Adult Prompts is used to assess ADHD symptoms in adults. The WJ IV is an intelligence test that evaluates a wide range of cognitive functions with three batteries: the WJ IV Tests of Cognitive Abilities, the WJ IV Tests of Oral Language, and the WJ IV Tests of Achievement. Finally, the ASQ is a socioemotional and developmental screening tool for children between birth and age 6.

7. B: Recognizing intersectional contexts of privilege and marginalization would best help engage the mother in treatment. Intersectionality considers each individual's privileged and marginalized status in terms of all intersecting sociocultural contexts (e.g., race, ethnicity, religion, socioeconomic background, education). Culturally responsive therapists consider the client and the counselor's intersectional identity's impact on the client's presenting problem, treatment engagement, and treatment adherence. Validating rather than refuting core cultural beliefs surrounding mental health stigma can enhance the therapeutic relationship. Exploring the influence of the biases toward the school's majority culture is not conducive to engaging the mother in treatment. Finally, it is essential to validate historical trauma (and not denote its incongruence), particularly the trauma's connection to here-and-now experiences, values, and assumptions.

8. D: A research study's inclusion-exclusion criteria are a methodological feature that considers ethnocultural variables (e.g., race, ethnicity, gender, and age). Inclusion criteria are characteristics of the subjects participating in the study, whereas exclusion criteria disqualify individuals from being included. External validity, or how well the results can be generalized to other settings, is contingent upon the characteristics of the study's participants. For example, a study concludes that certain foods and additives may impact symptoms of ADHD. However, if the study was only conducted with white adolescent females, it has limited value and thus cannot be generalized to the client, an African American 7-year-old male. The design of the study (whether it is quantitative or qualitative), outcome measures (i.e., symptom reduction), and the length of follow-up (i.e., the intervention effects over time) are crucial elements of a research study; however, only inclusion-exclusion criteria affect the study's generalization to ethnocultural groups.

9. A: The ACA Code of Ethics states, "Counselors recognize historical and social prejudices in the misdiagnosis and pathologizing of certain groups and strive to become aware of and address such biases in themselves or others" (ACA, 2014, Section E.5.c). Section C.2 addresses professional competence, stating, "Multicultural counseling competency is required across all counseling specialties, [and] counselors [must] gain knowledge, personal awareness, sensitivity, dispositions, and skills pertinent to being a culturally competent counselor working with a diverse client population" (ACA, 2014, Section C.2.a). Regarding assessment instruments, counselors must "use assessment as one component of the counseling process, taking into account clients' personal and cultural context" (ACA, 2014, Section E). Because there is the potential for bias in nearly all assessments, counselors must consider using multiple methods and multiple informants to reduce cultural biases. Finally, counselors avoid imposing their values, attitudes, beliefs, and behaviors onto the client, making option D incorrect.

10. B: The Individuals with Disabilities Education Act ensures that students attending public schools are identified and assessed in a nondiscriminatory fashion. If students meet qualifications, they are entitled to a free and appropriate public education. This federal law also grants parents the right to due process, which would allow the mother the right to challenge the client's placement or treatment. The US Department of Education Office for Civil Rights ensures equal access to public school education; it enforces federal laws prohibiting racial discrimination, including Section 504 of the Rehabilitation Act of 1973 and Title II of the Americans with Disabilities Act. The Special Education and Rehabilitative Services Act ensures that individuals with disabilities are integrated into society and that parents, teachers, and students receive special education support. Lastly, FERPA, also known as the Buckley Amendment, protects the privacy of educational records by giving parents the right to access and, if necessary, amend their child's academic records.

11. A: Planned ignoring involves deliberately ignoring a predetermined target behavior. In this case, the target behavior is interrupting. An extinction burst occurs when the client increases his maladaptive behavior (i.e., interrupting) to gain the mother's attention. If the mother does not consistently hold a firm boundary, the behavior is reinforced and becomes more difficult to extinguish. Behavioral activation is a cognitive-behavioral technique used to help clients initiate values-based activities to improved depressive symptoms. Negative reinforcement occurs when there is a behavioral change that happens with the removal of unpleasant stimuli. For example, a parent yells at their child to clean up, the client complies, and the negative stimulus (i.e., yelling) discontinues. Response cost is a consequence-based strategy for ADHD that involves taking away token reinforcers in the presence of negative behaviors. Token reinforcers can be exchanged for preferred activities (i.e., extra computer time). An example of response cost would be to remove a token each time the client interrupts.

12. A: Principles of operant conditioning include extinction, punishment, reinforcement, and stimulus control. With operant conditioning, learning occurs in the presence of behavioral consequences or reinforcement. Extinction happens when the reinforcer for that response is stopped, which lessens the possibility of the behavior's recurrence. Time-out is also known as time-out from reinforcement. When a child is sent to time-out, they are being removed from a situation that is reinforcing undesirable behavior. Classical conditioning entails paring a previously neutral stimulus with an unconditioned stimulus. Operant conditioning varies from classical conditioning in that operant conditioning involves using reinforcement or punishment to increase or decrease behavior. Punishment can be negative (e.g., taking away privileges) or positive (e.g., dispensing a noxious stimulus). Counterconditioning is a form of classical conditioning used to replace a negative emotional response (e.g., fear) with a stimulus that elicits a positive or pleasant response (e.g., happiness).

13. C: One component of social learning theory is modeling. The theoretical underpinnings of behavior management include contingency theory, social learning theory, and cognitive components. Social learning takes place when behaviors are observed, modeled, and imitated. Discrete trial training teaches a skill step by step and behaviorally reinforces successful approximations to an overall goal. Counterconditioning is the reversal of earlier learning. Finally, differential reinforcement is a behavioral modification principle used to stop undesirable behaviors by positively reinforcing desirable behaviors.

Case Study 10

1. C: According to the DSM-5, "The presence of emotional or behavioral symptoms in response to an identifiable stressor is the essential feature of adjustment disorders" (APA, 2013).

2. A: According to DSM-5, "Adjustment disorders are associated with an increased risk of suicide attempts and completed suicide" (APA, 2013). Poor concentration often accompanies anxiety-related disorders, but individuals with adjustment disorders are not at an increased risk of poor concentration. Individuals with neurocognitive disorders and individuals with substance/medication-induced sexual dysfunction may be at an increased risk for drug and alcohol misuse. Panic attacks are symptoms of anxiety and other mental disorders and are not a risk factor for adjustment disorders.

3. B: Donald Super's life-span life-space theory is based on the assumption that career development is an ongoing process. Super integrated the constructs of life roles (e.g., tennis player, volunteer, wife), self-concept (i.e., self-understanding), and career maturity (i.e., one's ability to master tasks associated with the corresponding stages of career development) into his career development theory. Sunny Hansen is known for her theory of integrative life planning, which focuses on integrating values and cultural influences (e.g., socioeconomic status, ethnicity, gender, spirituality) into one's work. Anne Roe's theory of personality development and career choice emphasizes the role of early childhood experiences on career development. Finally, Edgar Schein used the concept of career anchors to explain how one's personal beliefs and values serve as an impetus for career choice.

4. D: Acceptance and commitment therapy would help the client become more actively involved in values-related activities (e.g., playing tennis or volunteering as a big sister). The goal of acceptance and commitment therapy is to investigate the client's values and encourage the client to participate in life. It is a recommended therapy for chronic pain, which the client identified as a concern. Reality therapy focuses on creating a success identity that emphasizes the importance of one's need for love and the need to feel worthwhile. Narrative therapy assumes that the subjective account of one's life is socially, culturally, and politically constructed. Narrative therapists work with clients to reauthor or restory their lives to externalize the problem.

5. D: The Career Beliefs Inventory is based on John Krumboltz's learning theory of career counseling. It is designed to identify problematic beliefs that interfere with career decision making, including indecision and high aspirations. The Vocational Preference Inventory is used to identify an individual's Holland type, which is based on John Holland's theory of vocational personalities and work environments. The Career Orientations Inventory is used to determine the motives, values, and skills associated with Edgar Schein's career anchors. The Vocational Interest Inventory is based on Roe's personality theory of career choice.

6. B: One technique of solution-focused brief therapy is to ask the client about a time when her problem did not exist or was less severe; this technique is known as the exception question. Solution-focused brief therapy is a short-term, solution-oriented best practice used to help clients establish and reach goals by improving motivation and creating measurable behavioral change. Freudian psychoanalysis focuses on how a client's unconscious influences affect how they think, act, and feel. Eric Berne, credited with developing transactional analysis, used techniques such as script analysis to explore the interaction of ego states (e.g., parent, adult, and child). Gestalt therapists emphasize the integration of mind and body through an awareness of the present moment.

7. B: The Age Discrimination in Employment Act prohibits preemployment screening instruments from being used as a means for discriminating against those over the age of 40 rather than 50. The US Equal Employment Opportunity Commission bans employers from intentionally using personality tests and other selection procedures to discriminate against individuals based on religion, race, nationality, disability, sex, age, or color. Ethical guidelines for using personality tests, such as the Myers-Briggs Type Indicator, state that feedback and clarification must be sought when interpreting results. Test administrators must set aside time for questions and avoid biased terms indicating that a particular personality preference is "not desirable." Lastly, the ACA Code of Ethics states, "Counselors carefully consider the validity, reliability, psychometric limitations, and appropriateness of instruments when selecting assessments and, when possible, use multiple forms of assessment, data, and/or instruments in forming conclusions, diagnoses, or recommendations."

8. A: The Myers-Briggs Type Indicator is based on Carl Jung's theory of psychological type. The Strong Interest Inventory helps individuals identify careers based on interests. The Career Orientations Inventory is based on Edgar Schein's career anchors or career identities. The Ashland Interest Inventory is available to individuals with employment barriers, including certain educational, mental, cognitive, or physical conditions.

9. C: An interior decorator would give the client the highest job satisfaction of the careers listed if her code is SAE (social, artistic, enterprising). John Holland conceptualized six occupational and personality categories: realistic (R), investigative (I), artistic (A), social (S), enterprising (E), and conventional (C), or RIASEC. Holland used a hexagon to illustrate the positioning of each occupational category, with each point representing one of the Holland types. Work environments and personalities that are most similar are adjacent to one another. For example, the client is a teacher, which puts her in the social category. The social category includes career environments and personality types described as humanistic and responsible (e.g., teachers, nurses, social workers). Categories adjacent to social (i.e., artistic and enterprising) are more likely to include careers that would also be a good fit for the client. For example, interior design is grouped with the artistic category. Accountants are included in the conventional category, which is nonadjacent to social. Another nonadjacent category is the realistic category, which includes careers such as veterinarian. Lastly, systems analyst is included in the investigative category, which is also nonadjacent to the social category.

10. A: Existential therapy would best address the client's anxiety related to her professional identity and the search for purpose and meaning in her life. Existential therapists help clients create purposeful lives, learn to exist with themselves and others peaceably, and remove the anxiety blocking them. Behavior modification uses learning techniques (e.g., operant conditioning, aversive conditioning) to help clients make behavioral changes. CBT focuses on how a client's thoughts influence how they think and feel. Psychoanalytic theory is based on the assumption that there are unconscious influences that affect how a person acts or feels.

11. D: "I'm encouraged that you are committed to the process, but I can't help but notice the sadness you are experiencing today" is the statement that best reflects core counseling skills. The counselor acknowledges the client's underlying feelings, provides feedback grounded in the here and now, and allows space for the client to explore these feelings. Answer A is incorrect because it is an inaccurate account of what the client expressed. There was no discussion of divorce or the implication that it would affect all of her future career choices rather than the ones with lower pay. Answer B does not acknowledge the underlying feelings of sadness. Answer C is an example of a poorly timed and poorly constructed self-disclosure. When appropriately used, self-disclosures should promote client growth and leave clients with the feeling that they are understood.

12. B: The client is currently experiencing an unexpected transition. Schlossberg's categories of adult transition serve as the basis for her adult career development transitions model. An unexpected transition represents a change in one's relationships, roles, expectations, or responsibilities. For the client, this unexpected transition is caused by relational conflict and marital separation. An expected transition is a predictable or scheduled transition. An expected transition can be marriage, going to college, or retirement. A chronic transition or chronic "hassles" would describe frequent job loss, recurring medical problems, or unmanaged mental health conditions. Finally, a never-occurring or nonoccurring transition is an expected or scheduled transition that never happens (e.g., acceptance to graduate school, pregnancy).

13. A: The client is in the valuing phase of the CASVE decision-making model. The CASVE decision-making model uses a cognitive information processing approach (CIP) based on Frank Parsons' three-factor model. When individuals are in the valuing phase, they prioritize career options and construct a cost-benefit analysis of how a new career path fits into their values. The CASVE phases are communication, analysis, synthesis, valuing, and execution. In the communication phase, a career concern is identified by examining the gap between where one sees themselves and where one would like to be. In the analysis phase, there is an acknowledgment of a career problem and an investigation into how the problem can be resolved. This generally includes obtaining an understanding of oneself and one's viable career options. The synthesis phase involves elaborating on potential solutions and identifying areas consistent with one's values, abilities, interests, and knowledge. The execution phase is where one determines an action plan.

Case Study 11

1. A: A DSM-5 criterion for MDD includes "feelings of worthlessness or excessive or inappropriate guilt (which may be delusional) nearly every day (not merely self-reproach or guilt about being sick)" (APA, 2013). Recurrent thoughts of death and depressed mood also characterize MDD but are not associated with delusional thinking. An overestimation of impending danger occurs in the presence of agoraphobia, specific phobias, and other related conditions.

2. C: *Susto*, in particular interpersonal *susto*, is characterized by feelings of abandonment, loss, sadness, suicidality, and poor self-worth. According to the DSM-5, "*Susto* is an illness attributed to a frightening event that causes the soul to leave the body and results in unhappiness and sickness, as well as difficulties functioning in key social roles" (APA, 2013). The DSM-5 describes syndromic types to include interpersonal *susto*, *susto* relating to a traumatic event, and *susto* marked by somatic symptoms. *Ataque de nervios* (i.e., "attack of nerves") is an idiomatic expression used by Latinos to describe symptoms of intense anger, grief, worry, dissociation, or emotional distress. *Ataque de nervios* can escalate to the point of uncontrollable crying, seizures, shaking, and verbal or physical aggression. These attacks can occur as the result of a stressful event (e.g., news of the death of a significant person, familial conflict) but can also happen in the absence of a stressful event or trigger for a minority of individuals. *Confianza* is a Hispanic value that refers to the sense of comfort and ease when revealing oneself to another. For Hispanics, establishing trust within the confines of the therapeutic relationship can promote healing and restore ties within the context of personal relationships. Finally, *mal de ojo,* a Spanish term meaning "evil eye," is associated with social conflict or jealousy and is believed to cause physical illness, misfortune, and death.

3. C: The CFI does not include direct lines of inquiry for experiences of racism and discrimination. Found in Section III of DSM-5, the CFI uses clinically specific lines of inquiry useful for diagnostic and treatment planning purposes to include "Cultural Definition of the Problem (questions 1-3); Cultural Perceptions of Cause, Context, and Support (questions 4-10); Cultural Factors Affecting Self-Coping and Past Help Seeking (questions 11-13); and Cultural Factors Affecting Current Help Seeking (questions 14-16)" (APA, 2013). When inquiring about cultural factors affecting current help seeking, practitioners are encouraged to "elicit possible concerns about the clinic or the clinician-patient relationship, including perceived racism, language barriers, or cultural differences that may undermine goodwill, communication, or care delivery" (APA, 2013). However, the CFI does not ask directly about experiences of racism and discrimination.

4. D: Latinos place greater significance on supernatural forces than on nonspiritual forces. Latinos believe that spiritual influences include intermediary saints and other supernatural powers. In addition, Latinos place high importance on extended family, are more likely to use indirect communication, and emphasize collective harmony over personal fulfillment.

5. D: Using motivational interviewing, you would elicit change talk by evoking the client's optimism for change by asking about a previous change that she successfully made in her life. Motivational interviewing uses various techniques to reduce ambivalence and enhance motivation to change. The spirit of motivational interviewing focuses on collaborating with the client, evoking reasons for change, and honoring the client's autonomy. Helping the client reevaluate her relationship with her husband would not be aligned with the spirit of motivational interviewing because the client did not establish this as an area in need of change. Using persuasion and confrontation is not in alignment with the spirit of motivational interviewing. Exploring disadvantages of the status quo is a component of motivational interviewing; however, the counselor must guide the client in this process rather than confront the client to take action.

6. C: The ACA Code of Ethics defines social justice as "the promotion of equity for all people and groups for the purpose of ending oppression and injustice affecting clients, students, counselors, families, communities, schools, workplaces, governments, and other social and institutional systems." As such, promoting social justice is considered a core professional value for all certified counselors. Counselors must be aware of their client's uniqueness within the client's culture and within the counselor's own culture. Counselors must consider multiple ways that the intersectional identities of the client and counselor exist within the surrounding society. Professional integrity involves protecting and honoring the client-counselor relationship. Counselors are also called to honor diversity and embrace a "multicultural approach in support of the worth, dignity, potential, and uniqueness of people within their social and cultural contexts" (ACA, 2014). Lastly, beneficence is a professional value demonstrated when one is "working for the good of the individual and society by promoting mental health and well-being" (ACA, 2014).

7. D: You are providing congruence by remaining open to the client's underlying experiences in the present moment and responding authentically. Congruence (or genuineness) is expressed when counselors accurately attend to the interpersonal and intrapersonal aspects of the therapeutic relationship. Counselors need to be mindfully aware of their own intrapersonal experiences to skillfully respond to the client's experiences (i.e., the interpersonal facet). Increasing differentiation is a Bowenian family therapy technique. Bowen believed that optimal family functioning occurs with healthy boundaries or differentiation. Shaping competence is a technique used by structural family therapists when emphasizing the positive behaviors of family members. Positive reinforcement is a behavior modification technique used to increase desired behaviors.

8. D: Beck would attribute causes of the client's distorted thinking to their view of themselves, their world, and their future. These cognitive deficiencies are known as the "cognitive triad." Freud attributed maladaptive behavior to unresolved conscious conflicts. Adlerian therapists view maladjustment as the development of a mistaken style of life leading to feelings of inferiority. Known for rational-emotive therapy, Ellis suggests that irrational thinking can be deconstructed by recognizing an activating event, beliefs, and consequences.

9. A: Behavioral activation is a cognitive-behavioral approach for treating depressive symptoms, including those associated with social isolation. It works by positively reinforcing activities related to one's values and enjoyment rather than waiting for depressive symptoms to diminish before engaging in these activities. Motivational interviewing is used to reduce ambivalence and elicit change talk. Identifying concepts and faulty assumptions contributing to one's failure identity is associated with Adlerian therapy. Lastly, reality therapy suggests that one's "quality world" is at the core of life. One's quality world includes individuals we are closest to and those who supply us with satisfying experiences.

10. B: Interpersonal therapy is a form of cognitive therapy based on the assumption that depression is an illness rather than a moral failing. Interpersonal therapists operate on the premise that interpersonal problems fall into four separate categories: grief and loss (e.g., complicated bereavement), including trouble reestablishing social ties soon after the loss; a major life change or role transition; conflict in a valued relationship; or social isolation. Psychoanalytic therapy stresses the importance of discovering unconscious forces that drive behavior. Person-centered therapy uses the core facilitative conditions of unconditional positive regard, empathy, and genuineness. Finally, gestalt therapy focuses on successfully integrating the mind and body through present awareness.

11. B: Although all theoretical orientations can be adapted for use with culturally diverse populations, the core elements of person-centered therapy would best enable you to uphold professional ethical principles. According to the ACA Code of Ethics, "Counselors are aware of—and avoid imposing—their own values, attitudes, beliefs, and behaviors. Counselors respect the diversity of clients ... and seek training in areas in which they are at risk of imposing their values onto clients, especially when the counselor's values are inconsistent with the client's goals." The Association for Spiritual, Ethical, and Religious Values in Counseling provides a more thorough overview of ethical competencies aligned with the ACA Code of Ethics. Person-centered therapy is nondirective and uses the facilitative conditions of unconditional positive regard, empathetic understanding, and genuineness to guide the client toward self-actualization. Person-centered therapists respect diverse values, attitudes, and beliefs and refrain from taking the "expert role" in clients' lives. In general, behavior therapy does not consider the client's sociocultural background but instead views specific behaviors as a series of "maladaptive responses." Illegal in most states, conversion therapy is supported by conservative religious organizations that view same-sex attraction as pathological. Rational-emotive therapy is less likely to uphold ethical principles primarily because of the techniques "forcefully disputing" irrational thoughts in efforts to change "maladaptive behaviors." Unless adapted for diverse populations, rational-emotive behavior therapy (REBT) does little to consider the sociocultural and political influences on an individual's thoughts and behaviors.

12. C: Elizabeth Kubler-Ross's stages of grief are often cyclical rather than linear. While there are defined stages of grief, all individuals experience grief differently, with most moving back and forth between the stages of denial, anger, bargaining, depression, and acceptance. Cultural differences are found in varying practices, rituals, and beliefs that a person incorporates into cultural expressions of grief. Individuals in the second (i.e., anger) stage of grief may lash out and blame others for their loss. In the first (i.e., denial) stage of grief, individuals experience disbelief and shock, and in the fourth (i.e., depression) stage, individuals experience sadness.

13. C: Counselors are instructed to "refrain from referring prospective and current clients based solely on the counselor's personally held values, attitudes, beliefs, and behaviors. Counselors respect the diversity of clients and seek training in areas in which they are at risk of imposing their values onto clients, especially when the counselor's values are inconsistent with the client's goals or are discriminatory in nature" (ACA, 2014). The ACA Code of Ethics specifies that the client's failure to pay agreed-upon fees justifies appropriate termination. Counselors review policies and procedures associated with nonpayment as part of informed consent. In terms of counselor competence, the ACA Code of Ethics states, "If counselors lack the competence to be of professional assistance to clients, they avoid entering or continuing counseling relationships. Counselors are knowledgeable about culturally and clinically appropriate referral resources and suggest these alternatives. If clients decline the suggested referrals, counselors discontinue the relationship" (ACA, 2014). Lastly, counselors are ethically obligated to end professional counseling relationships when the client no longer benefits from counseling.

NCMHCE Practice Test #2

Case Study 1

PART ONE
INTAKE
<u>CLIENT</u>
Age: 9

Sex: Male

Gender: Male

Sexuality: Heterosexual

Ethnicity: Caucasian

Relationship Status: Single

Counseling Setting: Private practice clinic

Type of Counseling: Individual counseling with family involvement

Presenting Problem: Behavioral problems and social skills issues

Diagnosis: Autism spectrum disorder, without accompanying intellectual impairment (F84.0)

<u>PRESENTING PROBLEM:</u>

You are a private practice, licensed counselor. The client is 9 years old and comes to the first session with his parents. The client has been previously diagnosed with autism via use of the Autism Diagnostic Observation Schedule-Second Edition by a psychologist, and you receive supporting documentation for this diagnosis. The client demonstrates difficulties with normal back-and-forth communication with peers, difficulty maintaining eye contact during the session, and difficulty with imaginative play with peers as reported by his parents. The client and his parents also report what they call "OCD behavior"—for example, he often lines up toys and insists that they "have to be this way"—and that he has trouble with changes in schedule, often becoming aggressive toward the parents if changes occur. The parents report that he is very rigid and that certain activities and play have to be done a certain way or he becomes upset, which affect the home, social, and school settings. The client's intellectual quotient is above average for his age per the supportive testing provided. The parents report that the client's difficulty with changing plans or daily changes causes him to become angry and confrontational.

<u>MENTAL STATUS EXAM:</u>

The client is oriented to person, place, situation, and time. The client appears clean and is wearing season-appropriate clothing; however, his parents report that he often wears the same outfit for several days because he gets frustrated with having to change his clothes and showering. The client was minimally involved in the intake session and was instead focused on reading a video game walk-through book.

77

FAMILY HISTORY:

The client reports that his parents are supportive of his issues that are a result of autism. The client says that his 8-year-old brother gets frustrated sometimes because his parents often support the client and focus on him more due to his autism. The client reports that he does not have any friends.

1. You want to confirm the psychologist's diagnosis of autism spectrum disorder (ASD); therefore, you explore differential diagnoses. All of the following are differential diagnoses for ASD, EXCEPT:

    a. Intellectual disability (ID)
    b. Attention-deficit hyperactivity disorder (ADHD)
    c. Reactive attachment disorder
    d. Schizophrenia

2. The client appears uninterested in the session. Based on what you see, which of the following would be the most appropriate clinical intervention based on the client's diagnosis and presentation?

    a. You encourage the client to participate so that he can feel better.
    b. You talk with the client about the video game book he is reading.
    c. You continue talking with the parents because they are providing helpful information and you know that building rapport with the client will be a long process.
    d. You attempt to process with the client about why he is not engaging.

3. Which one of the following would be an appropriate referral to make for this client?

    a. Speech therapy
    b. Applied behavior analysis
    c. Occupational therapy
    d. Medication management

4. During the end of the session, the parents express concern about bills for these services, wanting to ensure that they pay them appropriately. When considering fees, which of the following is the most appropriate response when the payment amount for a session causes economic hardship for the client and they are unable to pay?

    a. The clinician will use a collection agency if fees cannot be paid.
    b. The clinician will inform the client about the use of a collection agency in the process of obtaining informed consent and will seek support from the agency when collection is needed.
    c. The clinician will inform the client regarding payments due and seek their payment prior to using the collection agency even when it was included within the informed consent.
    d. The clinician will write off the session as pro bono because this would best support the client.

5. All of the following would be indicated short-term goals for the client based on the information presented, EXCEPT:

    a. The client will learn social skills to improve social interactions with peers.
    b. The client will improve imaginative play skills in order to improve relationship quality with peers.
    c. The client will learn and implement coping skills for managing frustration when his schedule changes.
    d. The client will improve in his anger management skills.

78

PART TWO
THIRD SESSION, 2 WEEKS AFTER THE INITIAL INTAKE

The client comes to the session, sits down, and is quiet. The parents report that prior to the session he was playing an online game and became so upset that he threw his video game console. The parents express frustration that they do not know what to do when this happens. You provide psychoeducation to the client regarding coping skills to manage frustration. You find out that the parents respond by removing access to video games, and this usually results in yelling back and forth with the parents and the client. The parents do typically encourage the client to listen to music because this appears to be very effective in calming him down. The client expresses frustration with the people that he was playing with by saying that they "cheated and are lying about it." You support the client with cognitive reframing.

6. When the client becomes angry, the parents are unsure of what to do. Which of the following would be considered positive reinforcement of the client's behavior?

   a. The client does not become angry when he loses, and the parents provide praise.
   b. When the client resists becoming angry despite circumstances that usually generate his anger, the parents withhold a negative consequence (such as scolding) to encourage him to continue the appropriate behavior.
   c. The parents ignore the client when he throws his video game console.
   d. The parents remove the video game console and restrict his access to it over the next week.

7. All of the following are helpful therapeutic modalities for behavioral problems related to autism spectrum disorders, EXCEPT:

   a. Cognitive behavioral therapy (CBT)
   b. Dialectical behavior therapy (DBT)
   c. Behavior therapy
   d. Applied behavior analysis

8. Which of the following populations often responds best to eye contact being maintained most of the time?

   a. Caucasian
   b. African American
   c. Asian
   d. Native American

9. You do not believe that the kids the client was playing video games with were cheating, and you do believe that it is more likely that the client was losing and was upset for that reason. Which one of the following actions would likely be the most helpful response to the client?

   a. Process the situation with the client to help him take responsibility for his feelings and actions.
   b. Process the situation with the client to help him understand his feelings.
   c. Support the client in developing empathy skills to better understand the kids who he was playing games with.
   d. Validate the client's frustrations and support him in coping with his strong feelings.

PART THREE
SEVENTH SESSION, 5 WEEKS AFTER THE INITIAL INTAKE

This session is occurring in the client's home in order to observe behaviors in his natural environment. The client's parents and 8-year-old brother are present. You are observing during this session in order to gather information and then to provide psychoeducation at the end of the session to the parents. The client and his brother are sitting on the floor playing with a building toy, which the client's parents report is often a toy that causes him frustration because he plays very specifically with it and his brother does not want to play how he does. After about 5 minutes, the client becomes visibly frustrated as he is telling his brother to put a brick in a certain place because it is the same color and his brother says he is not going to and goes to build on his own. The client continues to build and asks for the piece repeatedly over a few minutes. The client then picks up what he is building and throws it against the wall and leaves the room.

10. Which of the following would be the most appropriate intervention with regard to providing treatment for this client's diagnosis?

   a.   Remind him of appropriate social skills.
   b.   Prompt him to play with another toy.
   c.   Encourage the client and his brother to play separately.
   d.   Prompt the client to take a break and listen to music to calm down.

11. During the session, the parents leave to answer a phone call, and the client's uncle comes into the room. When the client's uncle asks who you are and why you are in the home, which one of the following would be the most ethical response?

   a.   "I'm (state your name), your nephew's counselor."
   b.   "I'm a friend of the family; my name is (state your name)."
   c.   "I'm a counselor, but I can't say who I'm here to work with."
   d.   "I'm (state your name); it's nice to meet you. I can't answer that question, but you're welcome to ask your brother."

12. Based on the client's diagnosis of autism and his presentation throughout these sessions, which of the following areas of the mental status exam may be outside of normal limits?

   a.   Eye contact
   b.   Orientation to person, place, time, and situation
   c.   Hygiene
   d.   Memory

13. After the session, you provide psychoeducation to the parents regarding how to support their son in coping with the denial of his request to have a block put in a certain place. Based on your short-term goals with the client, all of the following would be appropriate interventions, EXCEPT:

   a.   Prompt the client to practice deep breathing.
   b.   Support the client to learn progressive muscle relaxation.
   c.   Remind the client that others have different ways of playing and that is okay.
   d.   Instruct the client on anger management skills.

Case Study 2

PART ONE

INTAKE

CLIENT

Age: 20

Sex: Female

Gender: Female

Sexuality: Heterosexual

Ethnicity: Asian

Relationship Status: Single

Counseling Setting: College counseling clinic

Type of Counseling: Individual counseling

Presenting Problem: Panic attacks

Diagnosis: Provisional diagnosis: panic disorder (F41.0)

PRESENTING PROBLEM:

You are a counselor working in a college counseling department. The client comes in after being late to class several times over the last month due to reported "freak-outs" in the morning. The client experiences the following panic symptoms: accelerated heart rate, sweating, shaking, shortness of breath, and a feeling of impending doom. The client reports a feeling of impending doom when she wakes up on days when she has classes, and this anxiety tends to escalate into fear of having a panic attack on a daily basis, often making her late to her first class. The client is worried that she will have panic attacks every day for the rest of her life. She says that her parents have put a lot of pressure on her to get a high grade point average at college. The client is worried about how this pressure and the panic attacks are going to affect her doing well at college and engaging socially.

MENTAL STATUS EXAM:

The client is oriented to person, place, time, and situation. The client does not appear anxious or depressed and was friendly and engaged.

FAMILY HISTORY:

The client reports that she is close with her parents but that they often have high expectations of her and that she worries about disappointing them. The client has an older brother who is 25 and is a lawyer. The client says some of the pressure is wanting to be as successful as her brother because she thinks her parents are really proud of him.

1. Although you suspect that the client has panic disorder, all of the following diagnoses or areas should be assessed as differential diagnoses, EXCEPT:

    a. The possibility of generalized anxiety disorder
    b. Whether the panic attacks are expected, unexpected, or both
    c. The possibility of major depressive disorder
    d. Cognitive processes that occur when experiencing a panic attack

2. Your client is worried about how panic attacks are affecting her academic life. With appropriate releases of information signed by the client, which of the following would be the most effective way to advocate on behalf of the client with the college based on her presenting needs?

    a. Meet with her teachers to discuss what the client is going through
    b. Meet with the college's department of disabilities to discuss leniency with attendance
    c. Meet with teachers of the classes that the client has in the morning to discuss extending deadlines for her assignments
    d. Meet with the college's department of disabilities to discuss extending deadlines for her assignments

3. All of the following are short-term goals for treatment for the first month of therapy, EXCEPT:

    a. Implementing calming and coping strategies for panic symptoms
    b. Providing psychoeducation on cognitive reframing
    c. Reducing the frequency and intensity of anxiety and panic attacks
    d. Processing aspects of the client's relationship with her parents

4. You provide psychoeducation on mindfulness activities to support the client in managing her morning panic attacks. All of the following are mindfulness strategies, EXCEPT:

    a. Coloring or drawing
    b. Deep breathing exercises
    c. Cognitive reframing
    d. Body scanning

5. Based on Shawn Shea's model for the clinical interview, which of the following statements is part of closing the intake session?

    a. "You've made a great choice for yourself by deciding to start therapy. I think that if we make a good plan together, we can improve management of your panic attacks."
    b. "It seems like your panic attacks are unexpected, but there are some things you can do to improve your management of them. I want you to read this literature on coping skills for panic symptoms."
    c. "Let's talk about panic disorder so you understand more about what's happening to you."
    d. "It was great meeting with you today! I think we can do some good work together. I'll walk you out to the lobby."

PART TWO

SECOND SESSION, 2 WEEKS AFTER THE INITIAL INTAKE

The client enters the room and appears distracted when she sits down because she has a furrowed brow and is looking off to the side of the room. You ask her what is on her mind, and she reports that this morning she had a panic attack that led to her throwing up. You ask her to talk through the moments when she noticed it starting and how the panic attack progressed. She says that she woke up and was worried that she might have a panic attack because she typically has one on school days, and this turned into worry that she might be late for class, which compounded into worry about how it might affect her grades and eventually into certainty that she would fail. The client then experienced an increased heart rate, chest tightness, difficulty breathing, a feeling of impending doom, shaking, and finally vomiting. You empathize with the client and provide psychoeducation on the management of panic attacks.

6. Which of the following would be considered a negative attending behavior?

   a. Leaning forward
   b. Consistently matching the client's posture and repeating her statements throughout the session
   c. Using hand gestures for emphasis
   d. Turning your body 30 degrees in relation to the client throughout the session to present a less aggressive posture

7. All of the following are helpful cognitive behavioral therapy (CBT) techniques to manage the anxious thoughts that lead to a panic attack, EXCEPT:

   a. Thought stopping
   b. Reframing
   c. Progressive muscle relaxation
   d. Radical acceptance

8. You had an argument with your roommate prior to the session and are distracted. Which of the following would be the most appropriate decision with regard to your client's well-being as it is impacted by your distraction?

   a. Reschedule the session with the client.
   b. Be aware of how your personal life is impacting the session and refocus as needed.
   c. Talk with the client about how you might impact the session and get refocused.
   d. Start the session a little late so you can resolve the argument in order to be more focused.

9. When this session is over, you check your online dating profile and notice that a past client's sister reached out to you showing interest in going on a date. You and this past client terminated 3 years ago. Which one of the following is aligned with the ethical guidelines of the American Counseling Association (ACA)?

   a. You did not have a counseling relationship with your past client's sister, so this does not prohibit you from dating her.
   b. You can proceed with a date because it has been 3 years since you worked with her sister.
   c. Document your decision and how the relationship is nonexploitative prior to going on a date with this client.
   d. You cannot date this person because she is related to a former client and 5 years have not passed since terminating the counseling relationship.

PART THREE

TWENTIETH SESSION, 22 WEEKS AFTER THE INITIAL INTAKE

You are meeting with the client for the termination session. You review the treatment goals and the client's progress. The client is no longer experiencing panic attacks, and she reports that she has felt panic attacks coming on but that she intervenes early and often to prevent them from occurring. You and the client have prepared for this date during the last few sessions in order to prepare the client for transitioning to independence from therapy. You and the client discuss her use of coping skills and natural supports to continue to manage panic symptoms. You also inform the client of how to reconnect if she needs to receive therapeutic support again and then terminate services.

10. All of the following are primary focuses of the termination session, EXCEPT:

   a. Signaling an end to the therapeutic relationship
   b. Encouraging ongoing therapeutic changes
   c. Identifying that growth has occurred
   d. Evaluating the effectiveness of therapy

11. Some clients may need to be referred to another counselor. All of the following are appropriate reasons to make a referral, EXCEPT:

   a. You fail to connect with the client due to personality differences.
   b. You do not specialize in the disorder experienced by the client.
   c. The client would benefit more from a psychiatrist or a medical specialist.
   d. The client and you have very different political affiliations, and their presenting problems relate to political events.

12. The client asks you if she could return to work with you after the termination session if panic symptoms were to worsen or return. Which one of the following is the most ethical response?

   a. Encourage her to continue to use coping skills learned in sessions, and assure her that you would be able to work with her should she have the clinical need for therapy
   b. There is nothing ethically wrong with working with this client again
   c. You would not be able to provide counseling services without bias and should refer the client to another therapist if she needed to reinitiate counseling
   d. The client should find a new therapist because you would be affected by bias if you reestablished the counseling relationship. But you can counsel her until she begins meeting with her new therapist.

13. You are supervising a counseling resident, and their established client has canceled several sessions in a row. Which of the following would you encourage the counselor to do?

   a. Follow up with the client to ascertain the reason for their cancellations.
   b. Cancel ongoing sessions until the client can commit to regular sessions.
   c. Contact the client to encourage them to trust the therapeutic process and continue to have sessions.
   d. Support the client by providing an option to have a referral if they think that counseling is not working.

Case Study 3

PART ONE
INTAKE
CLIENT
Age:

Client 1: Age 18

Client 2: Age 21

Client 3: Age 22

Client 4: Age 19

Client 5: Age 18

Sex: Male and female

Gender: Male and female

Sexuality: Heterosexual

Ethnicity: Multiracial

Relationship Status: All members are single

Counseling Setting: Counseling clinic

Type of Counseling: Group and individual counseling

Presenting Problem: All individuals are seeking support for struggles related to borderline personality disorder.

Diagnosis: Borderline personality disorder (F60.3)

PRESENTING PROBLEM:
You are a licensed therapist running a dialectical behavior therapy (DBT) group for young adults. You also provide a weekly individual counseling session for each group member, which is common practice for DBT group therapy. During the first session, you provide psychoeducation on DBT and the group process. Most of the members seem closed off and sometimes aggressive in response to being asked to speak during the first session, which can be consistent with borderline personality disorder. Client 3 becomes upset about halfway through the session, stating that he does not need to participate because the group will eventually end, so he does not need to build relationships with the group members. You end the session by planning individual therapy sessions with each group member.

MENTAL STATUS EXAM:
All clients appear to be oriented to time, situation, location, and person. The clients are all dressed appropriately for the weather. No clients appear to experience any visual or auditory hallucinations. Most of the clients are presenting as friendly but guarded.

FAMILY HISTORY:

Most of the clients report distressed relationships with their parents or guardians and that they have not had stable relationships throughout their lives.

1. All of the following are criteria for borderline personality disorder, EXCEPT:

- a. Recurrent suicidal behavior
- b. Binge eating
- c. Inappropriate, intense anger or difficulty controlling anger
- d. Recurrent depressive episodes

2. Which of the following is considered a differential diagnosis for borderline personality disorder?

- a. Reactive attachment disorder
- b. Conduct disorder
- c. Alcohol use disorder
- d. Post-traumatic stress disorder (PTSD)

3. Which of the following would be an appropriate short-term goal for the first month of the weekly therapy sessions?

- a. Identify the ways in which borderline personality disorder affects the individuals' relationships.
- b. Improve the relationship quality with people of importance to the individuals.
- c. Reduce client urges to engage in self-harming behavior.
- d. Improve communication skills with people of importance to the individuals.

4. Client 3 is resistant to the group process. Which of the following would be a helpful tactic in engaging the client?

- a. Process with the client about his feelings by taking him aside during the session, reminding him that other group members may feel similarly.
- b. Use dyads to encourage the client to share his feelings with a peer.
- c. Provide psychoeducation on the effectiveness of groups with borderline personality disorder.
- d. Encourage client 3 and the other clients to process their hesitancy about therapy.

5. All of the following are important factors when considering the setting of this counseling session, EXCEPT:

- a. Ensuring that the building's janitorial staff knows not to interrupt sessions when the door to your personal office is closed
- b. Sitting directly in front of the clients
- c. Providing different seating options within the office and allowing the client(s) to choose their own seat
- d. Minimizing outside distractions such as telephones

PART TWO

FIRST INDIVIDUAL SESSION, THE SAME WEEK AS THE INITIAL INTAKE

You meet with client 3 for his individual therapy session. The client continues to be resistant, stating that he does not need to meet with you. You spend the session trying to build rapport with the client and are successful in taking down some of his walls. The client says he knew client 2 from back when he was in high school and began telling you that she slept with a bunch of guys and did a lot of drugs. You redirect the client back to focusing on himself. The client starts to open up about his relationship with his parents growing up and how he thinks they did not really try to show him affection and this made him sad talking about it. The client concludes by saying "I feel overwhelmed sharing all of this because I've never talked about it before." You thank the client for sharing and you empathize with him.

6. Due to resistance, you choose to use motivational interviewing techniques with client 3. Which of the following would be an approach in engaging the client in treatment planning that uses motivational interviewing?

    a. You realize that you are imposing your goals for engagement, so you support the client in identifying what is important to him.

    b. You decide to support the client in reframing thoughts about counseling and its ability to improve his life.

    c. You realize that the purpose of the client's behavior is to escape counseling, so you continue to engage the client in order to prevent escape.

    d. You assess the client's personality by discussing birth order and its effects on functioning.

7. With new information about client 2, which of the following would be the most appropriate response to this information?

    a. Be aware of how this information affects your unbiased interactions with client 2.

    b. Keep this information in mind because it may help you support client 2.

    c. Bring this up when you have an individual session with client 2 to determine if it is true information.

    d. Explore why this information matters to client 3.

8. Which of the following statements demonstrates the use of empathy regarding the client's disclosure about his relationship with his parents?

    a. "It sounds like talking about this is difficult for you."

    b. "Correct me if I'm wrong, but it sounds like you didn't feel a connection with your parents growing up and this is hard to talk about."

    c. "I'm sorry to hear that you had little affection from your parents, but I'm proud of you for talking about it now even though it's hard."

    d. "I can imagine that it's hard to talk about something so personal and that it would be sad to not be close with your parents."

PART THREE

FIFTH SESSION, 5 WEEKS AFTER THE INITIAL INTAKE

You meet with the group and continue DBT psychoeducation regarding distress tolerance. About halfway through the group, you notice that client 4 has not shared much, and you ask her about this. The client states that every time she wants to talk, she cannot find a way into the conversation because others are talking. This group is in the working stage of group therapy, they are actively engaged in the session, and they are all also actively engaged in individual therapy.

9. In DBT, all of the following are main focuses of therapy, EXCEPT:

    a. Mindfulness

    b. Emotional regulation

    c. Distress tolerance

    d. Systematic desensitization

10. All of the following would provide space for client 4 to participate more, EXCEPT:

 a. Dyads
 b. Rounds
 c. Active listening
 d. Cutting off

11. All of the following are core concepts of distress tolerance in DBT, EXCEPT:

 a. TIPP
 b. A pros and cons list
 c. Self-soothing
 d. Thought stopping

12. During this session, client 1, who is a quieter member of the group, begins to cry and client 5 tries to rescue him by immediately providing comfort. Which of the following demonstrates the counselor's most therapeutic rescuing response?

 a. Allow client 5 to ease client 1's pain because this builds group cohesion and helps client 1.
 b. Encourage client 5 to allow client 1 to experience his pain.
 c. Support client 1 in engaging in coping skills to manage his strong emotions.
 d. Directly engage with client 1 using the skill of immediacy.

13. You suspect that client 1 is actually experiencing symptoms consistent with antisocial personality disorder. Which one of the following statements best characterizes antisocial personality disorder?

 a. Disregarding or violating the rights of others
 b. Argumentative/irritable/defiant behavior
 c. Grandiosity, lack of empathy, and a need for admiration
 d. Severe introversion that keeps the individual from participating in daily activities

Case Study 4

PART ONE
INTAKE
CLIENT

Age: Husband, 38; wife, 37

Sex: Husband, male; wife, female

Gender: Husband, male; wife, female

Sexuality: Husband, heterosexual; wife, bisexual

Ethnicity: Caucasian

Relationship Status: Married

Counseling Setting: Counseling clinic

Type of Counseling: Couples counseling

Presenting Problem: The couple is experiencing distress because the wife has had a sexual affair with a woman.

Diagnosis: Adjustment disorder, unspecified (F43.20) and relationship distress with spouse or intimate partner (Z63.0)

PRESENTING PROBLEM:

You are a licensed counselor meeting with a couple in your private practice clinic. The couple comes in, and they both sit down at far ends of the couch and do not look at each other. After explaining informed consent and other intake policies, you begin to ask the couple what brought them to counseling, and they both sit silently. You ask the couple if it is hard to start this conversation because of why they came, and they both nod. You ask the couple if it might be easier to start with how they met and why they fell in love with each other, and they both nod in agreement that they can talk about that. The couple appears more comfortable after this and even say a few statements to each other about shared experiences during the conversation. You circle back to the reason why they came to therapy, and the wife says that she assumes that she should talk first. She states that about a week prior she told her husband that she had an affair with a woman a few months before. She continues that, at the time, she was curious and it occurred while she was drunk and insists that it meant nothing. The husband states that he still loves her, but he is not sure how he is going to move past this. He emphasizes that not only did she have an affair, but her action exposed an aspect of her that he did not know about, making him question whether she even finds him attractive.

MENTAL STATUS EXAM:

The couple presents as withdrawn at the start of the session, but they open up as they talk about lighter subjects. Both individuals are oriented to person, place, time, and situation.

FAMILY HISTORY:

The husband and wife have been married for 13 years. They report that they met when friends introduced them and that they dated for about 2 years before getting married. The couple have two children: two daughters (ages 7 and 10). The couple reports that they have been in "parent mode" for the past few years and have not been emotionally connected to each other because their attention has been predominantly focused on their children.

1. Which of the following is a unique ethical consideration for couples counseling versus individual counseling?
   a. Autonomy
   b. Dual relationships
   c. Extensions of the counseling boundaries
   d. Professional competency

2. Which of the following is the most important area for you to focus on first when counseling this couple?
   a. Improving communication skills between the couple to facilitate conversations about how they got to this point in their marriage
   b. Processing how the couple got to this point to determine what the couple's needs are
   c. Stabilizing the couple's relationship so that the goals of counseling can be identified
   d. Exploring thoughts and feelings about the affair so that counseling efforts can be targeted

3. You supervise an intern in your clinic who is working with a couple that is in counseling for coparenting but is also in a legal battle for custody. Which of the following is the most ethically sound indication to release information for legal purposes?
   a. The husband's lawyer requests records of sessions, so you provide them to the lawyer because they are a legal representative and you have written consent to release the information.
   b. The court subpoenas the records, so you provide them without written consent from either individual.
   c. The wife's lawyer requests you to appear in court, so you attend and testify without written consent from either the wife or husband.
   d. Both individuals can request and receive records because they are both the identified client, and you must provide records when they are subpoenaed.

4. Which of the following assessments would be the most helpful in treatment planning for this couple?
   a. Relationship Assessment Tool
   b. Gottman Relationship Checkup
   c. Family APGAR assessment
   d. Love Language Quiz

PART TWO
THIRD SESSION, 3 WEEKS AFTER THE INITIAL INTAKE

The couple comes into the session and sits down. Their body language does not appear as uncomfortable as it has in previous sessions because they are sitting a little closer together. You ask both individuals what they need to work on. The wife says that she knows that she needs to rebuild trust, and the husband says that he wants to know more about what happened in the affair before they move forward. The couple report that they tried to engage in sex, but that the husband stopped during intercourse. The husband states that he could not get the idea out of his mind that his wife does not find him attractive because she was with a woman. You ask the husband what it means for their marriage if his wife does not find him attractive, and he states that it means he will not be able to please her. You then ask him what it means for the relationship if he cannot please her, and he responds that it means he cannot be a good husband. You follow up asking what it means if he cannot be a good husband, and he says that they will have a miserable marriage. You support effective communication strategies and empathize with the couple. After the session, the wife comes back to get her coffee that she left and says that she knows that she hurt her husband and is in the wrong, so she will do whatever her husband needs to rebuild trust.

5. At one point during the session, the husband stops talking completely. Which one of the following actions is the most effective way to deal with this example of stonewalling?

    a. Instruct the client to express that he is overwhelmed and to request a break.
    b. Instruct the client to walk away without saying something that would escalate the situation.
    c. Encourage the couple to discuss how they are feeling and address their presenting emotions and thoughts.
    d. Encourage the couple to support each other in coping with strong emotions and then help them process how they are feeling.

6. The Gottman Method focuses on having five positive interactions to every one negative interaction. Which of the following statements uses the Gottman Method approach of the positive-to-negative ratio?

    a. Take breaks in an argument to ensure that you mean what you say.
    b. Focus on small acts of love often.
    c. Focus on your friendship with each other.
    d. Communicate early and often to manage conflicts before they grow.

7. Which CBT technique did you use in the session summary when you responded to the husband's statement about not feeling that his wife is attracted to him?

    a. Downward arrow
    b. Radical acceptance
    c. Guided discovery
    d. Cognitive challenging

8. In order for you to assist in stabilizing this relationship, you must focus on building trust between the individuals. All of the following will help build this trust, EXCEPT:

    a. Improving conflict resolution skills
    b. Creating a safe environment for the wife to express her feelings
    c. Increasing positive interactions
    d. Increasing empathy

9. You are using narrative therapy with the couple. Which one of the following actions is an example of narrative therapy?

    a. Prompt the couple to read therapeutic books related to their problem areas.
    b. Provide homework for the couple to write a story together in order to work on collaborating and considering each other's viewpoints.
    c. Each individual writes a narrative of the story of their problem and then is guided in rewriting the story from a different, more positive, perspective.
    d. In a therapy session, each individual tells the story of their relationship from the view of a narrator in order to see things more objectively.

PART THREE
FIFTH SESSION, 5 WEEKS AFTER THE INITIAL INTAKE

The couple comes into the session and continues to appear more comfortable with each other. Both individuals report that they have been intentional about spending more quality time with one another. The husband says that his wife made sure that he had time to go fishing with his father last weekend, which meant a lot to him. During the session, you discuss events leading up to the affair and both agree that they have spent the majority of the last few years neglecting their relationship. The wife begins to speak but expresses that she knows she is the one who hurt her husband so she should not explain why it happened. You ask the husband if he wants to know how she is feeling and he nods. The wife explains that she felt he was not interested in her anymore, and although she knows what she did was not okay, she felt validated and cared for by the woman. The husband begins to cry. You continue to support the couple's exploration of this area of their marriage and provide empathetic listening.

10. When the husband is crying, all of the following are helpful techniques for the couple, EXCEPT:
   a. Practicing immediacy
   b. Allowing space for him to cry
   c. Redirecting to the wife with questions about her response to his crying
   d. Supporting the husband in using coping skills

11. The wife states that she felt her husband was not interested in her anymore and refers to this feeling returning when she tried to have sexual intercourse with him, which was not successful. Which of the following cognitive distortions best describes this thought process?
   a. Catastrophizing
   b. Jumping to conclusions
   c. Emotional reasoning
   d. "Should" statements/beliefs

12. Based on the topics discussed during today's session, which of the following would be the most appropriate homework assignment?
   a. Each individual will engage in a significant, loving act toward the other during the next week.
   b. The couple will engage in sexual intercourse twice over the next week in order to increase intimacy.
   c. The wife will ensure that the husband can go fishing again so he can feel validated.
   d. The couple will engage in conflict resolution skills when experiencing significant conflict.

13. While managing this couple's therapy, you are also supervising an intern at the clinic who is seeing their own clients. You have recently received several complaints regarding this intern that include talking on their phone during sessions, late progress notes, and inconsistent communication with clients. You think the intern is not responding well to feedback and has not tried to make changes. Additionally, several of the intern's clients have terminated their counseling services. Which of the following is the most ethical response in this supervisory relationship?
   a. Consider termination of the supervisor/intern relationship.
   b. Provide further coaching to improve their professionalism.
   c. Initiate termination of the supervisor/intern relationship.
   d. Sit in on a session to observe the intern's behavior.

Case Study 5

PART ONE

INTAKE

<u>CLIENT</u>

Age: 51

Sex: Female

Gender: Female

Sexuality: Heterosexual

Ethnicity: Caucasian

Relationship Status: Divorced and single

Counseling Setting: Local government mental health agency

Type of Counseling: Individual counseling

Presenting Problem: The client is experiencing a recent separation from her last partner who was verbally and physically abusive, and she is currently living in a domestic violence home.

Diagnosis: Major depressive disorder, recurrent episode, moderate (F33.1) and post-traumatic stress disorder (PTSD) (F43.10)

<u>PRESENTING PROBLEM:</u>

You are a licensed counselor working for a local government mental health agency in the counseling clinic. The client was referred to receive case management and counseling after experiencing homelessness due to leaving a physically and verbally abusive relationship with her last partner. The client is experiencing the following depressive symptoms: sadness more often than not, mental fogginess, suicidal ideation, insomnia, significant weight loss, feelings of worthlessness, and fatigue. The client experiences PTSD symptoms due to having experienced several abusive relationships, including recurrent distressing intrusive thoughts regarding the physical abuse, distressing dreams related to abuse, and physiological reactions (difficulty breathing, heart racing) when she goes near certain places that remind her of the abuse. She also explains that she has been avoiding triggers, believes that no one can be trusted, has an exaggerated startle response, and has had difficulty experiencing positive emotions. The client says that she does not know if therapy can help because she feels like these events have changed her and that she cannot get back to "normal."

<u>MENTAL STATUS EXAM:</u>

The client's affect is flat, and she is hunched over in the chair. The client is oriented to person, place, time, and situation. She reports no hallucinations, paranoia, or depersonalization/dissociation.

<u>FAMILY HISTORY:</u>

The client has three adult children: a daughter (age 32), son (age 30), and a second daughter (age 28). The client reports on and off relationships with her children historically because they did not want to be around these men, but that they have rekindled their relationships recently. The client has been married twice, and, in addition to her most recent partner (unmarried), all three men have been physically and verbally abusive toward her.

1. All of the following are appropriate assessment tools to explore differential diagnoses for major depressive disorder and PTSD, EXCEPT

    a. Adjustment Disorder-New Module 20
    b. Generalized Anxiety Disorder-7 (GAD-7)
    c. Adult ADHD Self-Report Scale
    d. Acute Stress Disorder Scale

2. What information would be the most important to guide the development of a treatment plan for this client within the scope of the counselor?

    a. Reported amount of sleep per night
    b. Reported frequency of trauma responses
    c. The client stating that she wants to make friends
    d. The client stating that she wants to find housing

3. Which one of the following specifies the level of severity of depression for this client?

    a. Suicidal ideation
    b. Effects on functioning in multiple settings
    c. Level of depressed mood reported
    d. Number of criteria met over the minimum criteria for diagnosis

4. All of the following are possible risk factors for suicide, EXCEPT

    a. Substance use
    b. Hopelessness about one's ability to change one's situation
    c. Recklessness with decision making
    d. The presence of depression

5. Based on the client's past relationships, which of the following would be helpful in understanding the client's relationship patterns?

    a. A genogram
    b. Clinician Administered PTSD Scale for DSM-5
    c. Relationship Assessment Scale
    d. Adult Attachment Interview

PART TWO

FOURTH SESSION, 3 WEEKS AFTER THE INITIAL INTAKE

The client comes into the session, sits down, and immediately begins to talk about one of her roommates in the domestic violence home that has been making her angry because the roommate comes into her room when the client is gone and borrows her personal hygiene items. The client continues to explain that she worries that the roommate might come in while she is sleeping, but that she has not done this yet. You process these feelings with the client and identify that when she was a child, her uncle would come into her room without her permission and sexually abuse her. The client also reported that one of her ex-husbands would enter their bedroom drunk at night and would often hit her while she was asleep. You and the client discuss how to make her environment feel safe and how to engage in cognitive reframing. You empathize with the client and validate her emotions.

6. Which one of the following statements would be the most beneficial cognitive reframe for the client's beliefs about her roommate that would address an approach from a reality perspective?

    a. "My roommate may actually do something bad, so I need to set some boundaries with her regarding my room."

    b. "Currently, my roommate hasn't done anything other than enter my space without permission and borrow things, so this isn't the same as my past experiences."

    c. "I should talk with my roommate about boundaries."

    d. "My thoughts aren't reality; therefore, I should distract myself using coping skills."

7. You disagree with the client's evaluation of her situation and want to support her. Which of the following would most support the client's presenting needs?

    a. Validate the client's feelings and thoughts in order to continue building rapport.

    b. Empathize with the client's thoughts and feelings and encourage cognitive reframing.

    c. Challenge the client's thoughts and beliefs.

    d. Encourage cognitive reframing in order to guide the client toward your conclusion about her thoughts and beliefs.

8. What kind of cognitive distortion is the client experiencing?

    a. Labeling

    b. Personalization

    c. All-or-nothing thinking

    d. Jumping to conclusions

9. The client brings up how she often avoids certain restaurants and stores because they remind her of arguments she has had with her past partners that led to her experiencing physical abuse. Which one of the following treatments would be most helpful in managing this avoidance?

    a. Exposure therapy

    b. DBT

    c. CBT

    d. Integrative therapy

PART THREE

SEVENTH SESSION, 6 WEEKS AFTER THE INITIAL INTAKE

The client comes to this session, sits down, and starts talking about how she met a man and talked to him for about an hour and was frustrated at the end of the conversation because she feels that he is "like everyone I've been with before." The client continues to explain that she knows these men are not good for her and that she wants something different, but she is still talking to him. The client becomes frustrated talking about this and begins crying and breathing heavily, stating that, "I am broken and can't have a healthy relationship." You support the client through her strong emotions and provide empathetic listening.

10. The client identifies that she has reasons to change and has a plan to change how she approaches relationships. Which of the following identifies the client's stage according to the transtheoretical model of change?

    a. Preparation
    b. Precontemplation
    c. Contemplation
    d. Action

11. The client inquires about circumstances in which you, as the counselor, are able to disclose information from your sessions with her. All of the following are true regarding disclosure of information, EXCEPT:

    a. You may disclose information to the client's insurance company because they are a payor.
    b. You may disclose information when the client expresses suicidal ideation with a plan and intent.
    c. You may disclose information when the client does not show up for a session because you are required to call the emergency contact.
    d. Even if the client is deceased, you cannot disclose information.

12. Based on the client's emotional reaction to talking about her relationship with this new man, which of the following would be the most clinically indicated response based on the client's stage of change?

    a. Validate the client's emotions and support her in engaging in coping skills.
    b. Challenge the client's cognitive distortion of labeling because the client is labeling herself based on past situations.
    c. Empathize with the client to build rapport.
    d. Validate the client's emotions and support her beliefs because she has had difficult relationships and this would be the most genuine response.

13. The client explains that she is having difficulty paying for her session and requests to trade the produce she grows in exchange for the cost of her sessions. All of the following are ethical considerations for bartering, EXCEPT:

    a. The possibility of exploitation or harm
    b. Which individual in the counseling relationship initiates the idea of bartering
    c. Whether, upon researching and identifying the monetary value of the trade, the costs match the value of therapy
    d. Whether this is a common practice in the community

Case Study 6

PART ONE

INTAKE

CLIENT

Age: 30

Sex: Female

Gender: Female

Sexuality: Heterosexual

Ethnicity: Caucasian

Relationship Status: Married

Counseling Setting: Counseling clinic

Type of Counseling: Individual counseling

Presenting Problem: The client is engaging in restrictive eating daily. The client engages in bingeing when her husband is away for business trips and engages in exercise as compensatory behavior.

Diagnosis: Anorexia nervosa, binge eating/purging type, moderate (F50.02)

PRESENTING PROBLEM:

You are a licensed counselor working in your own private practice, and you specialize in eating disorders. The client comes to counseling after her primary care physician (PCP) provided a referral to counseling due to restrictive eating that has led to a low body mass index of 16.5. The client says that she has lost about 30 pounds over the past 6 months and that she still feels that she is overweight. The client says that she usually consumes about 500 calories each day and that she fears that if she eats more, she will gain weight. The client's mother, who was overweight, passed away at age 46 due to an aneurysm, which has contributed to the client's perception that her mother's death was weight related. The client expresses that she also has a fear that if she gains weight, then her husband will not love her. She describes experiencing anxiety resulting from the belief that she is currently overweight and is therefore already at risk of both her husband not loving her and of dying. The client says that she generally restricts eating when her husband is home, but when he is on business trips she binges and then forces herself to throw up.

MENTAL STATUS EXAM:

The client is oriented to person, place, time, and situation. She reports no hallucinations or paranoia. The client was engaged in the session, but she had trouble accepting that her weight and self-talk were problematic.

FAMILY HISTORY:

The client has two siblings: a younger brother (29) and an older sister (32). The client says that her older sister is obese and she is worried that her body would deal with food similarly, causing her to gain weight easily if she ate more. The client has been married for about 1 month at this point and has lived with her husband for about 6 months total. She says that she feels pressure from her husband to be thin, and although he places this expectation on her, she says that she has felt this way prior to meeting him, but has lost more weight since they have been living together.

1. All of the following referrals are appropriate based on the anorexia bingeing/purging type diagnosis, EXCEPT:

    a. Dentist
    b. Psychiatrist
    c. Nutritionist
    d. Inpatient treatment

2. You are focusing on building a therapeutic relationship with the client. Which of the following terms focuses on viewing the client as the expert of herself and responding warmly with acceptance of where the client is in her life?

    a. Congruence
    b. Unconditional positive regard
    c. Mutuality
    d. Identification and internalization

3. Which of the following would be appropriate homework following the intake session?

    a. Complete a daily food log.
    b. Recommend that the client read a book regarding anorexia.
    c. Encourage the client to try foods that she thinks are off limits and to write down thoughts and feelings that she is experiencing when doing so.
    d. Ask the client to create a hierarchy of internal and external triggers for bingeing and purging.

4. Which of the following areas would be indicated to assess for in addition to eating disorders?

    a. Trauma
    b. Anxiety
    c. Depression
    d. Relationship quality

5. All of the following are considered differential diagnoses for anorexia nervosa, EXCEPT:

    a. Bulimia nervosa
    b. Social anxiety disorder
    c. Dependent personality disorder
    d. Hyperthyroidism

PART TWO
FIRST SESSION, 1 WEEK AFTER THE INITIAL INTAKE

You meet with the client in your office 1 week after the intake session. The client reports that her husband was out of town for half of the past week and she engaged in bingeing and purging. You review the client's food log with her and can see the difference between when her husband is home and when he is gone based on her documentation. The log included the client's thoughts following bingeing, purging, and restricting, and you and the client work on creating new scripts for the thoughts that have led to unhealthy eating and compensatory behaviors in the past.

6. You want to demonstrate congruence with the client when she begins to cry, and you feel the urge to sit beside her and put your hand on her shoulder to comfort her. Which of the following is the most important consideration?

   a. Handshakes are the only appropriate physical touch with a client.
   b. The appropriateness of this action depends on the sexual orientation and identified gender of you and the client, so as to not send the wrong message to the client.
   c. You must first consider if you want to comfort the client physically for your own needs or for the client's needs.
   d. Physical comfort is a typical human reaction, and this can build therapeutic rapport.

7. The client's food log has the following statement: "I'm not worth anything if I get fat, and I'm going to die." All of the following are more rational ways of reframing this thought, EXCEPT:

   a. "The reality is that I could get fat, which may result in my husband's unhappiness and my own death, but I can be healthy and keep this from happening."
   b. "Although being overweight isn't healthy, my worth isn't defined by weight."
   c. "My body isn't letting me down, and my husband loves me."
   d. "My worth isn't defined by my weight, and there are ways that I can be healthy to reduce my chances of dying younger than I want to."

8. The client's thoughts of worthlessness if she is overweight and that she will die as a result represent which of the following cognitive distortions?

   a. Personalization
   b. Always being right
   c. Emotional reasoning
   d. Overgeneralization

9. Which one of the following drugs has been proven beneficial in treating anorexia nervosa?

   a. Fluoxetine (a selective serotonin reuptake inhibitor [SSRI])
   b. Diazepam (a benzodiazepine)
   c. Amitriptyline (a tricyclic antidepressant)
   d. Olanzapine (an antipsychotic)

PART THREE

TWENTY-SECOND SESSION, 30 WEEKS AFTER THE INITIAL INTAKE

You meet with the client, and she comes and sits down and appears happy because she is smiling and sitting with an open posture. The client's food log shows improvement in engaging in healthier eating habits and minimal restriction. You and the client review her progress in treatment and agree that she has met all of the treatment goals. The client reports several situations in which she wanted to restrict, purge, and binge, but instead she engaged in cognitive reframing and was able to manage her reaction to the trigger. You praise the client and express that she should be proud of herself for her management of her symptoms. The client reports that she has gained weight and is in a healthy weight range at this point. She continues that her husband has made comments of concern about her weight gain and that the frequency of sex has decreased recently. The client says that she and her husband have been arguing about her eating recently and that she does not feel that he supports her in recovering from her eating disorder. You empathize with the client.

10. You are frustrated because the client's husband does not support her progress. Which one of the following is the most appropriate first response?

    a. You encourage the client to invite her husband to another session in order to discuss his frustration with her weight gain.

    b. You support the client in developing communication skills to discuss her progress and health with her husband.

    c. You and the client discuss coping skills in order to help her cope with her husband's expression of frustration.

    d. You provide a referral for couples counseling.

11. Which of the following indicates that this client is ready for termination?

    a. The client reports that no symptoms of the eating disorder or trauma are present, and you also observe no symptoms.

    b. Minimal symptoms of the eating disorder and trauma are present, and the client manages them when they occur.

    c. The client has nothing to talk about in sessions and reports that she does not have anything she needs to work on.

    d. The client states that she is not restricting, bingeing, or purging and that she and her husband are going to start couples counseling.

12. The client expresses that she is afraid of termination and concerned that she might "fall back into unhealthy eating behavior." Which of the following might be most helpful to provide to the client?

    a. Provide results of weekly screenings to encourage her because she has made significant progress.

    b. Provide referrals to support groups so the client is connected to others who experience similar symptoms.

    c. Express to the client that you are proud of her accomplishments and that she will do great following termination.

    d. Reassure the client that you are available to restart sessions if she needs support in managing symptoms.

13. All of the following are ethical considerations for termination, EXCEPT:

    a. You have different values than the client, so you consider termination and referral.

    b. It is apparent that the client no longer needs counseling.

    c. The client has not paid the agreed-upon counseling fees, so consideration of termination is appropriate.

    d. The therapist is at risk of harm by the client.

Case Study 7

PART ONE

INTAKE

CLIENT

Age: 25

Sex: Male

Gender: Male

Sexuality: Bisexual

Ethnicity: Caucasian

Relationship Status: Single

Counseling Setting: Telehealth

Type of Counseling: Individual counseling

Presenting Problem: The client is experiencing difficulty focusing on work due to a childhood diagnosis of attention-deficit/hyperactivity disorder (ADHD) and thinks that if he cannot keep up with work, he is going to get fired.

Diagnosis: Attention-deficit/hyperactivity disorder (ADHD), predominantly inattentive presentation (F90.0)

PRESENTING PROBLEM:

You are a licensed counselor working in your own private practice and providing telehealth sessions to clients. The client states that he is having trouble keeping up with tasks at work. The client reports that he wakes up and does not want to go to work because he knows he will not get much done. The client is often late to work, and although he is typically the only one in the office, his employer comes to work every now and then, and he worries that he will get caught arriving late. He says that he procrastinates on tasks but, often near the end of the day, finds motivation to complete the tasks and stays late to do so. In addition to his trouble at work, the client says he thinks that he does not do much that makes him happy. He expresses the desire to write stories and play guitar more because these activities used to make him happy, but he has trouble finding motivation to engage in them at the present.

MENTAL STATUS EXAM:

The client is oriented to person, place, time and situation. The client is engaged and participates fully in the intake session. The client does not appear anxious. The client has a flat affect.

FAMILY HISTORY:

The client reports a strained relationship with his parents, but he says that he does not want to talk about them because they are not the reason that he is in therapy. The client says that he has a younger sister (age 23) and that they are not close. The client reports that he currently has a girlfriend.

1. The client self-reported his ADHD diagnosis, and you want to confirm this diagnosis. All of the following are appropriate steps to take to confirm the diagnosis, EXCEPT:

   a. As a licensed therapist, you are authorized to diagnose ADHD like you would diagnose other mental health diagnoses.
   b. You collaborate with the client's PCP to diagnose the client.
   c. You request records from the client related to the diagnosis in order to confirm it
   d. You give a provisional diagnosis of ADHD in order to continue to assess for ADHD on your own.

2. Which of the following would be the most appropriate short-term goal to focus on first in therapy for this client?

   a. Encourage the client to invite his girlfriend to a session so they can work through how ADHD affects their relationship.
   b. Identify current ADHD behaviors that cause the most difficulty for the client.
   c. Learn and implement planning and organization skills.
   d. Identify, challenge, and reframe self-talk that reinforces behaviors associated with ADHD.

3. Which of the following assessments would be the most effective in evaluating ADHD for this client?

   a. Vanderbilt ADHD Diagnostic Rating Scale
   b. An organizational assessment
   c. Vineland Adaptive Behavior Scales
   d. Conners Abbreviated Symptom Questionnaire

4. Which of the following differential diagnoses should be considered for this client?

   a. Generalized anxiety disorder
   b. Specific learning disorder
   c. Substance use disorder
   d. Major depressive disorder

5. You have been diagnosed with ADHD and experience similar struggles that you want to share with the client. Which one of the following is the most helpful description of effective self-disclosure?

   a. Sharing personal experiences can enrich the counseling relationship.
   b. No level of self-disclosure is appropriate because you are counseling the client and do not want to risk them having to support your emotional needs.
   c. You use self-disclosure in order to develop rapport with your client.
   d. You use self-disclosure when it is beneficial for displaying your empathetic understanding and when it benefits the counseling relationship.

PART TWO

THIRD INDIVIDUAL SESSION, 3 WEEKS AFTER THE INITIAL INTAKE

You meet with the client, and he reports that he was able to improve his productivity by organizing his day based on organization techniques that you discussed in therapy. The client says that he really wants to focus on getting into writing stories again and that he also wants to learn to play guitar. He explains that his attempts at learning guitar are disrupted because, when he tries, he becomes frustrated, stops quickly, and often does not revisit playing for weeks. You ask the client about thoughts that he has that are a barrier to writing and playing the guitar, and he identifies that he often anticipates that he will just get frustrated and stop, so there is no point in trying. You support the client in cognitive reframing.

6. You were approached by a local community college to speak to a therapy group that is provided for students regarding management of ADHD. All of the following are American Counseling Association (ACA) considerations for media presentations, EXCEPT:

a. Your statements must be based on accepted counseling literature and practice.
b. It is made clear to the group that you are not establishing a counseling relationship with them.
c. Your statements align with the ACA Code of Ethics.
d. If you do not have training as an educator, you must decline to meet with the group.

7. Which of the following is a helpful goal following this session to support the client in writing and playing the guitar more often?

a. Identify goals that are easily achievable within the week.
b. Identify goals that are slightly difficult in order to push the client.
c. Recommend that the client choose two nights this week to play guitar for at least 30 minutes.
d. Refocus the goals back to management of ADHD because this is why the client came to counseling.

8. Some of the client's sessions are being provided via telehealth. All of the following are unique considerations for telehealth sessions that are different than in-person sessions, EXCEPT:

a. Body language
b. Cost
c. Orientation to person, place, time, and situation
d. Confidentiality

9. You suspect that the client might have depression. Which one of the following statements is a helpful cognitive reframing of the client's statement of "I will get frustrated and won't enjoy playing guitar, so I won't play at all"?

a. "I might enjoy playing guitar; therefore, I'll try to play for a few minutes."
b. "I should wait until tomorrow, and I'll play guitar at 6 pm after dinner."
c. "I will play guitar when I'm ready, which is when I feel a bit more motivated."
d. "I might enjoy playing guitar more than I think I will because if I don't change what I'm doing, then things will stay the same."

PART THREE
TENTH SESSION, 16 WEEKS AFTER THE INITIAL INTAKE

It has been 1 month since you last saw the client because he has canceled many sessions in a row without explanation. You process attendance with him and then ask him for updates regarding how symptoms have been over the last month. The client says that there were many reasons for cancellations, such as going to dinner with friends, being too tired, and forgetting about the session and making other plans. The client says that he got a new job and states that he is doing much better managing his ADHD symptoms in the new position. You and the client process what was difficult about his last position and then identify that these tasks are not present in the current position. A majority of this session was spent assessing the level of symptomatology experienced over the past month and the client reporting on events that occurred since the last session.

10. Which of the following is the most therapeutic manner of determining the root of the client's inconsistent attendance?

    a. Asking the client, "Why have you been canceling sessions?"
    b. Reviewing progress toward goals
    c. Asking the client, "What is most important to you for us to be working on in sessions?"
    d. Discussing scheduling to determine if the time or frequency is not working for the client

11. Due to the client's inconsistency in attending sessions, which one of the following areas might you focus on in order to improve his attendance?

    a. Goals that are meaningful to the client
    b. Different or additional diagnoses
    c. Organization skills
    d. Scheduling conflicts

12. During several sessions, you have noted in your mental status exam that the client demonstrated psychomotor activity. Which of the following might be a common psychomotor activity for someone who has ADHD?

    a. Fidgeting
    b. Scanning/excessive eye movement
    c. Posturing
    d. Pacing

PART FOUR
TWENTY WEEKS AFTER THE INITIAL INTAKE

Following the 10th session, the client has not responded to your attempts to contact him and the only communication from the client has been the cancellation of the 11th session.

13. Which of the following would be the most ethical response to the client's lack of communication regarding cancellations?

    a. You terminate services because the client is participating voluntarily and if he does not want to attend, then he does not have to.
    b. You attempt to reach out several times to provide contact information and referral information.
    c. You continue to attempt to make contact with the client until a response is provided.
    d. You reach out after the first no-show, and then you wait for the client to make contact to initiate services again.

Case Study 8

PART ONE
INTAKE
CLIENT

Age: 45

Sex: Male

Gender: Male

Sexuality: Heterosexual

Ethnicity: Caucasian

Relationship Status: Divorced, single

Counseling Setting: Private practice

Type of Counseling: Individual counseling

Presenting Problem: The client is experiencing difficulty in functioning in all areas of his life due to inhalant use.

Diagnosis: Inhalant use disorder, severe (F18.20)

PRESENTING PROBLEM:

You are a licensed counselor working in a private practice. You specialize in substance use disorders. The client comes into the session, is very friendly, and states that although his sessions are court ordered, he wants to get help with his inhalant use. The client spent the first half of the session explaining what happened to lead to him getting his third charge of driving under the influence of inhalants. The client says that he had twin sons 13 years ago and they both were in the ICU; one of his sons died after about a month. The client began drinking alcohol to excess daily for about 6 months, which then transitioned to inhalant use. The client says that he uses contact cement, model glue, paint, and permanent markers to become intoxicated. The client identified the following symptoms of inhalant use disorder: increase in frequency and amount of use over the past 5 years, several failed attempts at cessation of inhalant use, craving inhalants throughout every day, losing several jobs because of his inability to get to work on time due to inhalant use, use that has affected his ability to have visits with his children and maintain employment, use that increases the risk of harm to himself and others such as driving under the influence, increased tolerance, and continued use even when he knows it is negatively affecting his life. The client wants to become sober, improve his relationship with his children, and maintain employment.

MENTAL STATUS EXAM:

The client is oriented to person, place, time, and situation. The client does not appear to be under the influence of inhalants because he does not display any symptoms of use. The client is friendly and engaged in the session.

FAMILY HISTORY:

The client has three sons that are 11, 13, and 16 years old. The client is divorced as of 3 years prior and reports a contentious relationship with his ex-wife due to his difficulty following through with visits with their children. The client and his ex-wife were married for 17 years and dated for about

5 years before they were married. The client states that he loves his ex-wife but that she has currently been dating another man for the past 2 years and he knows they likely will not reconcile. He says that he understands why she does not want to be with him, and he thinks that he is not good for her or his children at this time.

1. The client's sessions are court ordered. Which of the following is the most therapeutic course of action with regard to sharing information with the court?

    a. Take steps to get written consent from the client, attempt to limit information given to the court, and/or prohibit the release of information if possible.

    b. Provide all of the information that the court requests per the legal requirements.

    c. Provide minimal information to protect your counseling relationship with the client.

    d. Restrict access to the client's records; even though therapy is court ordered, it does not mean that the court has access to all documentation.

2. When considering treatment goals, all of the following are indicated areas to explore, EXCEPT:

    a. Grief or trauma regarding his son's death

    b. Depression symptoms that may lead to inhalant use

    c. His relationship with his ex-wife

    d. Barriers to maintaining employment

3. You suspect that the client has post-traumatic stress disorder (PTSD). Which of the following does not meet the criteria for PTSD?

    a. Difficulty with memory surrounding the traumatic event

    b. Poor concentration

    c. Irritability

    d. Symptoms occur after at least 3 days following the traumatic event

4. To better understand the client's behavior and relationship patterns, which of the following would be the most useful?

    a. Conduct a mental status exam during each session.

    b. Complete a genogram.

    c. Assign the client homework to complete a thought log regarding inhalant use and his relationships.

    d. Request a release of information in order to communicate with the client's ex-wife to get input on his behavior.

5. When discussing the informed consent form, you cover the risks of counseling. Which one of the following is NOT an expected risk of counseling?

    a. Therapy can make the client feel worse initially.

    b. The client may need to meet with multiple counselors prior to finding a match.

    c. The counselor might not have the skill set needed to best provide benefit for the client.

    d. The client might choose to discontinue therapy earlier than recommended.

PART TWO

SIXTH SESSION, 3 WEEKS AFTER THE INITIAL INTAKE

The client comes into the session and looks tired, as evidenced by the darkness under his eyes and he is walking slowly. The client starts talking immediately about 2 days prior when he went to his ex-wife's house to pick up his kids for a visit and she told him that although she cannot stop this visit, due to recent inhalant use a few weeks ago, she talked with her lawyer about changing the status of his future visits to supervised visits, and she will be returning to court to do so. The client says that he spent time with his kids and that when he left, he stopped by a store to get acetone and that he used this substance that night. The client expresses guilt and shame surrounding using, which led to him using the acetone the next day. The day after he used inhalants, the client stated that he was thinking, "I already broke my sobriety; I may as well huff so that I can feel better." You empathize with the client regarding the situation because you can see how this would be distressing for him. The client says that his children seem bored when they are with him, as if they want to go home, which induces feelings of shame and sadness.

6. Regarding the client's thoughts after the second day of using inhalants in a row, which of the following would be the most appropriate cognitive reframe of this thought?

    a. "I broke my sobriety and need to focus now on how to get back on track."
    b. "I got off track, but I can make better choices in order to improve my situation by contacting my sponsor and counselor."
    c. "I may not be able to improve my relationship with my ex-wife or have the visitation agreement that I want. I just need to keep moving forward."
    d. "I can contact my lawyer and begin working on the visitation agreement so that I can manage future stress and will be less likely to feel that I need to use inhalants."

7. Which of the following cognitive distortions best defines the client's statement of "I already broke my sobriety; I may as well huff so that I can feel better"?

    a. Emotional reasoning
    b. Jumping to conclusions
    c. Magnification
    d. Mental filters

8. All of the following are possible symptoms of inhalant use, EXCEPT:

    a. Euphoria
    b. Nystagmus
    c. Muscle weakness
    d. Insomnia

9. Which one of the following best defines acceptance and commitment therapy?

    a. Notice and embrace the situation at hand.
    b. Accept the situation and realize one's ability to change thoughts and behaviors for a different outcome.
    c. Focus on human abilities and limitations.
    d. Focus on releasing repressed emotions and experiences.

PART THREE

FOURTEENTH SESSION, 7 WEEKS AFTER THE INITIAL INTAKE

You meet with the client after he requested an emergency appointment. The client says that he had a supervised visit with his children and he had used inhalants prior to the visit because he was anxious. The supervisor noted the intoxication and ended the visit early. The client says that this was 3 days ago and that he has used inhalants several times daily since the visitation. Due to his intoxication at the visit, all future visits have been canceled until the next hearing in court regarding visitations. The client says that he has been very depressed and that is why he is using inhalants. During the session, the client asks if he can go to the lobby to get water and you tell him that this is fine. The client returns, sits down, and appears listless because he is not displaying any emotion and has a very flat affect. You suspect that he is now intoxicated.

10. You want the client to know that you are listening because he is expressing strong emotions and you want to support him. All of the following demonstrate therapeutic listening, EXCEPT:

a. Mirroring
b. Attentive silence
c. Refraining from the use of "mm-hmm" and similar responses
d. Identifying and discussing verbal/nonverbal inconsistencies

11. If you suspect that the client may be intoxicated, all of the following are important considerations, EXCEPT:

a. Continuing or ending the session
b. Transportation home
c. Processing the client's intoxication
d. Termination with the client

12. Following this session, you determine that the client is not benefiting from therapy with you because he has used inhalants since at least your third week of sessions and almost daily since then. Which of the following would be the most appropriate intervention for this client based on his recent inhalant use?

a. Referral to another counselor
b. Psychiatric hospitalization
c. Inpatient drug rehabilitation
d. Case management from a local government agency

13. The client's probation officer requests session progress notes from the time with your client due to it being court-ordered therapy. Which one of the following statements is true regarding court-ordered therapy?

a. You must provide the requested documentation because this is court-ordered therapy and you are working under the discretion of the court in this situation.
b. The client does not retain any rights in court-ordered counseling.
c. You must request a release of information form from your client prior to releasing documentation.
d. Although the client does not retain rights, you try to receive informed consent anyway in order to retain the therapeutic relationship with the client.

Case Study 9

PART ONE

INTAKE

CLIENT

Age: 9

Sex: Male

Gender: Male

Sexuality: Heterosexual

Ethnicity: Caucasian

Relationship Status: Single

Counseling Setting: Private practice

Type of Counseling: Individual counseling

Presenting Problem: The client has been engaging in behavior that has gotten him suspended from school several times over the past year, which also causes significant distress for the client's family at home.

Diagnosis: Conduct disorder, childhood-onset type, with limited prosocial emotions, severe (F91.1)

PRESENTING PROBLEM:

You are a professional counselor, and you specialize in working with children and adolescents. The client comes to this session with his parents. You review informed consent with the client and his parents and begin to ask the client about what brings him to counseling. The client responds by saying "shut the hell up" and leaves the room to go to the lobby. The client's father gets up and follows him out, and after a few minutes they return. The client sits down and faces away from you. The client does not engage in the intake session aside from cursing at his parents when they report specific behavioral incidents and he disagrees with them about the facts of the events. The client's parents say that he has had "bad behavior" over the past 2 years and that his behavior has "gotten worse" over the past 5 months. The parents outline the following behavioral problems that the client engages in, in all settings: bullying, physical fighting, kicking and throwing items at his dog, intentionally breaking others' property, lying to others to get items or have access to activities, stealing items from others, truancy, and leaving the house at night without permission or supervision.

MENTAL STATUS EXAM:

The client was minimally engaged in the session. The client's behavior was withdrawn, argumentative, and labile.

FAMILY HISTORY:

The client has two younger brothers who are 6 and 7 years old. The client often engages in physical fights and arguments with his younger siblings and often will break or steal their toys. The client takes advantage of his 6-year-old sibling by conning him out of items and activities by convincing him that a certain trade or decision is better for him, when it is usually better for the client. The client's parents report that these behaviors occur at school and that the client does not have any friends as far as they are aware. The client's parents state that the client is adopted and that he was in foster care from when he was 2 until he was 4 years old. The client's parents state that his basic needs were neglected because his birth mother was heavily using drugs.

1. Which one of the following would be considered a differential diagnosis for conduct disorder?

    a.   Reactive attachment disorder
    b.   Major depressive disorder
    c.   Antisocial personality disorder
    d.   Autism spectrum disorders

2. It will be important to build rapport with this client to provide effective counseling. Which of the following would most effectively promote therapeutic rapport with this client?

    a.   Rapport will be built over time, so continue to be consistent and creative with your sessions.
    b.   Empathize with the client's view of why he engages in these behaviors.
    c.   The client is young; therefore, the parents will likely be the ones using interventions so it is more important to have rapport with the parents.
    d.   Spend a few sessions trying to play with the client.

3. All of the following treatment modalities and services would be appropriate based on the client's presentation, EXCEPT:

    a.   DBT
    b.   CBT
    c.   Family therapy
    d.   Medication management

4. Which of the following is an appropriate assessment tool to confirm the client's diagnosis of conduct disorder?

    a.   Delinquent Activities Scale
    b.   Conners Continuous Performance Test
    c.   Diagnostic Interview for Children and Adolescents
    d.   Child Behavior Checklist

5. All of the following are part of the Mental Status Exam (MSE), EXCEPT:

    a.   Thought process
    b.   Insight
    c.   Memory
    d.   Diagnosis

PART TWO

FOURTH SESSION, 4 WEEKS AFTER THE INITIAL INTAKE

You meet with the client alone, and he appears to be more comfortable with you because he comes in and starts talking about a video game that he plays. You share that you have played that video game before. During the session, the client mentions that his parents got his first report card of the year and found out that he was failing most of his classes. He started to say that he was worried that his dad was going to hit him because of his grades. You ask if his father hits him often, and he replies that he does several times a week. You try to inquire about the manner of hitting his father uses because a certain level of corporal punishment is legal in the state that you work in. The client says that he is not going to talk any more about this. You remind the client that you likely will need to report this to child protective services and he says, "I don't care" in response. You spend the rest of this session processing his relationship with his parents, and he discloses that he does love them, but that they are not his real parents. You meet with the client's parents near the end of the session, and, while talking with them, they report that he was neglected while in foster care because the foster parent was "just in it for the money."

6. Based on the client's report that his father hits him several times each week, which would be the next step based on best practice?

    a. Assess to determine if the abuse allegations are credible before reporting them to the relevant authorities.

    b. Gather the necessary information and report it to the relevant authorities regardless of whether or not the allegations seem credible.

    c. Request that the parents join the session to further process the allegations and determine their credibility.

    d. Continue to check in with the client during the next few sessions to determine if you can gather more substantial information before reporting any abuse to the relevant authorities.

7. Based on the information discussed in this session, you decide to begin supporting the parents in improving their son's attachment with them. All of the following would be beneficial homework assignments, EXCEPT:

    a. Assigning intentional one-on-one activities with each parent and the client

    b. Assigning reading homework for the parents regarding positive attachment

    c. Creating a reward system for behavior to create consistency and structure

    d. Having intentional weekly family time

8. In structural family therapy, there are subsystems within the family system. All of the following are subsystems, EXCEPT:

    a. The parents

    b. The client

    c. The younger siblings

    d. Social family members

9. The client becomes upset at the end of this session after talking about the alleged physical abuse, and he begins to throw toys and any items within arm's reach. Which one of the following would be the least helpful response when considering the client's current emotional state?

    a. Attempt to process the client's present thoughts and emotions.

    b. Use an open body posture and a calm voice.

    c. Disengage with the client with regard to the subject at hand.

    d. Use the 5-4-3-2-1 grounding technique.

PART THREE
EIGHTH SESSION, 8 WEEKS AFTER THE INITIAL INTAKE

Since the fourth session, child protective services investigated the client's abuse allegations and determined that they were unfounded. You discuss this with the client and he says he was lying because he was mad at his parents that day. You praise the client for being forthright today regarding the allegations and discuss how false allegations can be incredibly harmful to others and can strain his relationship with his parents further. You and the client process several situations similar to this in which he avoided responsibility. You empathize with the client and support his reflection on his behavior.

10. From a behavior therapy perspective, which of the following would best define what the client does when he blames others for his actions?

a. Escape
b. Attention
c. Item/activity
d. Sensory needs/stimulation

11. The client is resistant to making changes to his behavior. Which of the following conversations might you have with the client to encourage more appropriate behavior?

a. Assist him in identifying how he often receives negative consequences. Reiterate that the consequences of his actions do not make him happy, so it is worth trying something different.
b. Discuss the reward system to see if it can be made more motivating.
c. Empathize with the client regarding his desires and help him identify that more appropriate behavior can help him get what he wants more so than what he is doing now.
d. Continue the current course of treatment because you have developed a good rapport and he continues to participate; therefore, he will be ready to make changes when the time is right for him.

12. Which of the following cognitive distortions is often associated with anger?

a. Personalization
b. "should" statements
c. Disqualifying the positive
d. Catastrophizing

13. The client's parents have not paid for the past three sessions. All of the following are important considerations, EXCEPT:

a. Inform the client in a timely fashion of your intention to use a collections agency.
b. Offer the client the opportunity to pay for the past three sessions.
c. The policy should be covered in your informed consent document, and you should follow the agreed-upon terms.
d. Waive the session payments because the client is unable to afford them and you want to preserve the counseling relationship.

Case Study 10

PART ONE

INTAKE

CLIENT

Age: 24

Sex: Male

Gender: Male

Sexuality: Heterosexual

Ethnicity: African American

Relationship Status: Single

Counseling Setting: Private practice counseling clinic

Type of Counseling: Individual counseling

Presenting Problem: The client comes to counseling for help in managing anxiety, workplace dissatisfaction, and a pornography addiction.

Diagnosis: Generalized anxiety disorder (F41.1), other problem related to employment (Z56.9), religious or spiritual problems (Z65.8)

PRESENTING PROBLEM:

You are a professional counselor, and the client comes to counseling to work on anxiety, work dissatisfaction, and a pornography addiction. You and the client discuss his anxiety, and he identifies that he experiences anxiety at work, regarding daily tasks, and in social settings. The anxiety is characterized by restlessness, difficulty concentrating, muscle tension, and insomnia. The client states that at work he is often treated poorly by his supervisors, who often point out what he does wrong and do not acknowledge what he does right. He does not feel that he does as much wrong as they claim, and he often finds that their accusations do not accurately reflect his actions, which is frustrating. The client states that he has had many meetings with his supervisors and that they do not appear to try to understand his point of view. The client appears uncomfortable and begins to speak but stops for about a minute before saying that he also has a pornography addiction. The client says that he is a Christian and that he does not feel he should view any pornography, but also that he uses pornography a lot and does not feel like he has control over himself or the frequency at which he uses it. The client asks if you are a Christian, and you decide to disclose with him that you are, knowing this is an important part of the client's life and perspective. The client states that his work problems and pornography use are his most pressing issues.

MENTAL STATUS EXAM:

The client is oriented to person, place, time, and situation. The client appeared hesitant when talking about pornography use.

FAMILY HISTORY:

The client has a close relationship with his parents and his older sister. The client has close friends.

1. Although pornography addiction is not a DSM-5 diagnosis, based on what you know about the client, which of the following is the most likely reason that he engages in frequent masturbation?

    a. Anxiety
    b. Self-esteem
    c. Loneliness
    d. Obsession/compulsion

2. The client inquires about his counseling records when you are explaining informed consent. Which of the following statements is the most accurate with regard to the client's records?

    a. You can share session notes with your counseling resident for educational purposes because they are practicing under your license.
    b. When the client requests his records, you must provide full access to the records and support their interpretation as needed.
    c. Client records must be kept for at least 5 years before being appropriately destroyed.
    d. The counselor must make reasonable precautions to ensure the privacy of client records in the event of termination, incapacity, or death.

3. All of the following are hormones released during masturbation or sex, EXCEPT:

    a. Oxytocin
    b. Testosterone
    c. Dopamine
    d. Cortisol

4. Which of the following would be an appropriate short-term goal for this client that could be completed in the next month?

    a. Decrease the client's urges to masturbate.
    b. Explore what the client has liked and disliked about his current and past jobs.
    c. Identify and implement assertiveness skills in the workplace.
    d. Learn and implement coping skills for anxiety.

5. The client requests behavioral changes that can help reduce the frequency of masturbation. All of the following behavioral interventions can support a reduction in the desire for masturbation, EXCEPT:

    a. Exercise
    b. Spending time with family or friends
    c. Blocking pornographic websites
    d. Focusing on improving self-esteem

PART TWO

FOURTH SESSION, 4 WEEKS AFTER THE INITIAL INTAKE

You meet with the client and review a log that he brings in that documents how often he masturbated over the past week. The client's log showed that he masturbates about three to four times per day. The client appears to masturbate more when his roommates are not in the apartment and late at night when his time is less structured. The client reports that he has a job interview in a few days at a nonprofit agency that works with children to ensure that they have clothing. He feels that this will be meaningful work and is encouraged because he knows the supervisor there from a previous job, and he thinks that the supervisor is a respectful person. The client expresses worry that he will not be competent at the job based on how he is doing at his current place of employment. You support the client with reframing his anxious thoughts about the interview.

6. Based on the data gathered regarding the factors that lead to masturbation, all of the following would be possible interventions to manage these urges, EXCEPT:

    a. If possible, leave the bedroom to be with his roommates or go for a drive.
    b. Call a friend from his Bible study if he feels the urge to masturbate.
    c. Read the Bible or pray.
    d. Use the aversion therapy technique in which the client snaps a rubber band on his wrist when he feels the urge to masturbate.

7. Which of the following best describes the client's worry that he will not perform well at the new job opportunity based on his current employment?

    a. Fortune telling
    b. Catastrophizing
    c. Overgeneralization
    d. Emotional reasoning

8. The client often appears embarrassed when talking with you about masturbation. All of the following could be helpful in increasing the client's level of comfort with this conversation, EXCEPT:

    a. Immediacy
    b. Self-awareness
    c. Normalizing
    d. Summarizing

9. You complete a mental status exam during every session. Which one of the following domains would most likely be affected by the client's presenting diagnoses?

    a. Eye contact
    b. Mood
    c. Suicidality
    d. Orientation

PART THREE
TENTH SESSION, 10 WEEKS AFTER THE INITIAL INTAKE

The client comes into the session smiling and says that he is excited to share his log this week. The client shares that he masturbated an average of one to two times daily and that he even went a day without masturbating. You express your excitement for the client achieving his goals. Through processing, the client identifies that he refrained from masturbating most often by leaving his bedroom and finding something to structure his time late at night. The client says that he had difficulty refraining from masturbating mostly when he came home from a difficult day at work, or when he struggled to sleep. You and the client discuss calming techniques to use when he is stressed after work. You also recommend approaches to address difficulty sleeping. On days when the client masturbates, he explains that he often decides that since he already messed up, he can do it again. The client says that he is happy at his new place of employment and that it is just a hard job. You support the client in challenging his past cognitive distortion that his future employment experiences will be the same as his past experiences.

10. The client is engaging in all-or-nothing thinking with regard to his rationalization of masturbating again if he has already done so. Which of the following would be the most helpful reframe of this thought?

    a. "I did mess up, but I'm only human, so I won't beat myself up over it."
    b. "I didn't meet my goal, but this doesn't have to affect the rest of my day."
    c. "What happened can't be changed, so I'll just continue to move forward."
    d. "I'll take some time to do yoga to disconnect from this event and move forward with my day."

11. Which of the following is the most accurate definition of mindfulness?

    a. Meditation focused on being aware of thoughts and feelings and interpreting what those thoughts and feelings mean to you
    b. Being aware of how you feel in the moment and then engaging that awareness through the use of cognitive reframing
    c. Meditation focused on being aware of thoughts and feelings, being present in the moment without judgment or interpretation, and using grounding techniques such as deep breathing
    d. Using deep breathing, progressive muscle relaxation, and radical acceptance of how you feel and what you are thinking

12. All of the following can negatively affect sleep quality, EXCEPT:

    a. Alcohol
    b. Melatonin
    c. Exercise
    d. Drinking water around bedtime

13. You are reviewing this case with a counseling resident, and she does not think that the client is doing anything wrong by masturbating because it is a typical part of human functioning. You encourage your resident to remember all of the following in regard to this client, EXCEPT:

    a. The importance of supporting the diversity of clients
    b. Refraining from imposing your own values and beliefs on clients
    c. That the client is not causing himself any harm by refraining from masturbation
    d. That although you can encourage different viewpoints, you cannot impose them

Case Study 11

PART ONE

INTAKE

CLIENT

Age: 30

Sex: Female

Gender: Female

Sexuality: Heterosexual

Ethnicity: Pacific Islander

Relationship Status: Single

Counseling Setting: Private practice counseling clinic

Type of Counseling: Individual counseling

Presenting Problem: The client and her boyfriend recently broke up, and she is "tired of being with the wrong guys." She admits that she will often stay in relationships even if she knows they are wrong for her.

Diagnosis: Provisional diagnosis: Dependent personality disorder (F60.7), personal history (past history) of spouse or partner violence, physical (Z69.11), and personal history (past history) of spouse or partner psychological abuse (Z91.411)

PRESENTING PROBLEM:

You are a professional counselor working in a private practice clinic. The client comes in and sits quietly. The client appears nervous because she avoids eye contact and waits for you to initiate conversation. You ask why she is in counseling, and she responds that she is just tired. You ask more about this, and she says that she is not ready to talk about it yet. You decide to cover demographics and other less intimidating topics and then ask if she is comfortable talking yet. The client says that she feels a little more comfortable. She begins to state that she and her boyfriend broke up the previous week and that she was with him for 2 years. She explains that she has been "in this type of relationship before," continually finds the "wrong guy," and that she always goes "all in" with her relationships. Through processing, she identifies the following behaviors and beliefs: difficulty making daily decisions without the input of her partner, doing anything to gain support and affection even if she does not want to do the task or activity, quickly moving on to another relationship when a relationship ends, feeling that she cannot care for herself when she is not with someone else, and acknowledging that she needs others to take responsibility for major areas of her life. The client says that she has experienced physical and psychological abuse from partners, but that she is not ready to discuss this. The client identifies that her most important goal is to not end up in "the same relationship" again or rush into a relationship that is not right for her. Throughout the session, you provide empathetic and active listening. You suspect that the client has dependent personality disorder.

MENTAL STATUS EXAM:

The client is oriented to person, place, time, and situation. No hallucinations, delusions, or paranoia are reported. The client was anxious at the start of the session, but she was able to calm herself down by easing into the counseling relationship.

FAMILY HISTORY:

The client is close with her parents and her younger brother (28 years old). The client says that she was engaged twice before but that neither engagement progressed to marriage because her two fiancés both felt that she was too clingy and unable to care for herself.

1. Which of the following assessment tools would be used to best support the diagnosis of dependent personality disorder?

    a.   Minnesota Multiphasic Personality Inventory-3 (MMPI-3)
    b.   Rorschach inkblot test
    c.   Symptom Checklist 90-Revised (SCL-90-R)
    d.   Likert scale

2. When considering differential diagnoses, which of the following personality disorders might present similarly to dependent personality disorder?

    a.   Antisocial personality disorder
    b.   Histrionic personality disorder
    c.   Schizoid personality disorder
    d.   Obsessive-compulsive personality disorder (OCPD)

3. Some ethical standards can be altered based on the situation. Which of the following ethical standards would you likely not compromise on with this client?

    a.   Fees
    b.   Boundaries
    c.   Release of the client's records to her
    d.   Interpretation of assessment results

4. The client is hesitant about sharing her experiences of physical abuse. How does this inform your course of treatment?

    a.   Allow the client a few sessions to become more comfortable, and then strongly encourage the client to talk about the physical abuse.
    b.   Encourage the client to talk about the abuse during the intake session, and remind her that the more you learn about her, the more effective treatment will be.
    c.   Allow the client the space needed to become ready on her own, and bring it up every few sessions to check in and see if she is ready.
    d.   Check in every session to see if the client is ready to talk about the physical abuse, and then strongly encourage it when you think you have a strong therapeutic rapport with her.

5. Psychodynamic therapy has proven to be effective in the treatment of dependent personality disorder. Which one of the following is a defining principle of psychodynamic therapy?

    a. Childhood experiences and unconscious wishes and fears greatly shape an adult's personality

    b. Focusing on the present moment using mindfulness techniques to accept thoughts and feelings without judgment

    c. Changing the narrative from "I'm a loser" to "my anxiety sometimes makes me think I'm a loser"

    d. Using free association and dream interpretation to investigate conscious and unconscious thoughts

PART TWO

SIXTH SESSION, 6 WEEKS AFTER THE INITIAL INTAKE

The client comes in, sits down, and immediately says that she has been thinking and decided that she is now ready to talk about the physical abuse that she has experienced. She recounts that from age 18 until age 20 she was with a boyfriend who would smack her if she said something he did not like. She believes this is why she is so preoccupied with pleasing others. The client's second relationship was when she was 25 with a man who would get drunk nightly and punch her in the stomach or in the back when he was upset. You empathize with the client and reflect her emotions regarding these events. The client states, "I didn't deserve it when the drunk guy hit me, but I do feel I wasn't the best girlfriend with the first guy. I often didn't do enough for him and often said the wrong thing." Throughout the session, the client was tearful and started shaking slightly when speaking several times. The client paused for long periods before sharing more difficult parts of the story. You decide to assess for PTSD during this session, but she does not meet the criteria. When closing the session, the client states that she is not able to pay for today's session until the end of the week. The client has no history of nonpayment with you thus far.

6. All of the following are considerations that influence the reporting of abuse, EXCEPT:

    a. The age of the client

    b. The cognitive ability of the client

    c. Having insufficient information about the abuse

    d. The client asking you not to report the abuse

7. Which answer below best defines the level of responsibility that the client should take regarding physical abuse?

    a. The client can learn what to do differently next time as a girlfriend to avoid abuse.

    b. The client can acknowledge that she did not always do things correctly, but she did not deserve to be abused.

    c. The client can acknowledge that she did not deserve to be hit, but that the second abuser was under the influence so he should not have to take full responsibility for his actions.

    d. The client should not take any responsibility for being abused.

8. Your informed consent includes fees for nonpayment and late cancellations of sessions. Which of the following is the most therapeutic response to the client's inability to pay for the session until the end of the week?

a. Allow the client until the end of the week to pay for the session and waive the nonpayment fee.

b. Consistency with fees is important in the client–counselor relationship. The fee should still be applied, and payment is still expected on time.

c. Allow the client until the end of the week to pay for the cost of the session with the added fee.

d. Waive the session fee and nonpayment fee because the client is experiencing financial hardship.

9. At the end of this session, the client gives you a gift card to a restaurant because it is the last time you will see this client before Christmas. Which one of the following is the most appropriate clinical response considering ethics and your client's needs?

a. Accepting gifts is never appropriate, and you decline the gift.

b. Accepting gifts with a value of greater than $50 is inappropriate, so you decline the gift.

c. You accept the gift because it is not high in value and because the client's culture would view this rejection as offensive.

d. Based on the presenting problems, you decline the gift.

PART THREE

SEVENTH SESSION, 7 WEEKS AFTER THE INITIAL INTAKE

You meet with the client, and she reports that she started dating someone. You and the client spend some time talking about the man who she is dating and agree that he sounds like a nice person that is not taking advantage of her personality. You and the client discuss her having an increased awareness of the behaviors that she has engaged in in the past that she did not like. The client identifies that she has engaged in behavior that worries her with this boyfriend. She went out for lunch and felt compelled to buy him lunch also, even though he was not there. After exploring why the client feels an obligation to buy her boyfriend lunch when he is not present with her, it becomes clear that it is motivated by the fear that he will be offended that she bought herself lunch without thinking of him. You support the client in identifying more helpful thoughts related to this and ask her to complete a behavioral experiment regarding this situation. The client becomes frustrated that she is still struggling with relationships and says, "I think I'll just date who I want and how I want from here on out. It's definitely the easiest choice instead of doing all of this." You remind the client that therapy takes some time but can be really beneficial and you praise her for engaging fully so far.

10. Using the ABC model, the client's belief that her behavior will be offensive leads to all of the following consequences, EXCEPT:

a. Her boyfriend being happier in the relationship

b. Buying lunch more often for her boyfriend even if he is not around

c. Anxiety if she is unable to buy her boyfriend lunch

d. Her own perceived reduction in anxiety when she buys her boyfriend lunch

11. Which of the following statements demonstrates the use of paradox in response to the client's statement that she should just date who she wants?

   a. "You can continue to date who and how you want to; that is your own choice."
   b. "What if you decided to try things differently this time because you haven't been happy in the past with dating."
   c. "Maybe you should date who you want and how you want, even though it can be frustrating for you. This process does seem like a really hard step for you."
   d. "Only you can decide if you want to continue counseling; you can always take a break or wait until you're ready to work on your relationships."

12. Which of the following would be an appropriate behavioral experiment regarding the client's fear of offending the man who she is dating by not buying him lunch?

   a. The client will buy herself lunch this week and use thought processing techniques to manage her own anxiety.
   b. The client will buy herself lunch this week and use coping skills to show herself that she can be okay if she does not buy him lunch.
   c. The client will ask her boyfriend about whether or not it offends him when she does not buy him lunch.
   d. The client will buy herself lunch this week and not buy her boyfriend lunch to see if her assumption is true.

13. Using the psychoanalytic approach to analyze the client's statement about doing what she wants, you want to determine the influence of the id, ego, and superego. Which one of the following is the best definition of the Freudian concept of the id?

   a. Focus on unconscious basic impulses of aggression and sex.
   b. Focus on morals and ideals.
   c. Focus on the balance between morals/ideals and basic impulses.
   d. Focus on beliefs about the client's own functioning.

Answer Key and Explanations for Test #2

Case Study 1

1. C: Reactive attachment disorder is not a differential diagnosis for ASD. Reactive attachment disorder is often caused by insufficient care from a primary caregiver and is characterized by limited seeking of comfort or wants when distressed, limited positive affect, and unexplained irritability, sadness, or fearfulness. ID, ADHD, and schizophrenia are all appropriate differential diagnoses for ASD. ID can also present as a delay in development; however, it differentiates itself in older children because social skills are not as impacted as they are with ASD. ADHD can be similar to ASD due to attention difficulties, but these difficulties are secondary to the child's hyperactivity. Schizophrenia with childhood onset can present similarly to ASD because social skills can be impacted in the early phases of this condition.

2. B: You engage with the client about what he is reading because you want to create a connection and this is a very simple one to make. Encouraging the client to participate might work, but it does not create a connection with the client. You have learned a lot about the client from his parents, but you also need to engage him in building a therapeutic relationship. Processing with the client regarding his lack of participation may be helpful, but considering his diagnosis and age, it would be more helpful to talk with him about the video game book.

3. D: Medication may be helpful in managing the client's anxiety regarding situations in which he experiences rigidity. Because prescribing medications is outside of the scope of the counselor, a referral to a psychiatrist for medication management would be necessary. Occupational and speech therapy are more helpful with individuals with autism spectrum disorders that have intellectual deficits. Applied behavioral analysis is helpful for individuals with autism who experience behavioral issues but who also have trouble engaging in cognitive counseling; therefore, this client would not be a candidate for applied behavioral analysis.

4. C: The most ethical consideration according to the ACA Code of Ethics is providing an opportunity for the client to make a payment prior to seeking a collection agency (ACA Governing Council, 2014). Using a collection agency is ethical if the client is informed of this in the informed consent process and if they have been provided a chance to pay the fees. Writing off the sessions as pro bono should not be the first consideration because you want to settle on a payment rate that the client can pay prior to considering providing services for free.

5. B: The client will have difficulty improving imaginative play due to his diagnosis of autism spectrum disorder. The client would benefit from developing his social skills, coping skills for frustration management, and anger management because he has trouble tolerating change and because of his anger regarding rigidity and changes in his schedule.

6. A: The parents are providing positive reinforcement when they provide praise when the client exhibits appropriate behavior. The parents removing a consequence (scolding) to increase appropriate behavior is negative reinforcement. The parents ignoring a behavior is considered extinction. The parents removing the console would be considered punishment for his behavior.

7. B: DBT can be helpful for many different mental health disorders, but it is not proven to be beneficial in behavioral interventions for autism spectrum disorders. Cognitive behavioral therapy (CBT), behavior therapy, and applied behavior analysis are all beneficial in treating behavior issues related to autism.

122

8. A: When conducting clinical interviews, it's important for the counselor to practice cultural sensitivity. While blanket generalizations cannot be presumed across ethnicities, there are general cultural norms that have been studied, which can be grouped as high-context and low-context cultures. While no cultural demographic can be considered exclusively high or low, there are tendencies that have been identified. Low-context cultures, which generally include Caucasian Americans, utilize communication that is characterized as being blunt and direct and are more comfortable with direct eye contact when communicating. Words are the primary source of meaning in this form of communication. Conversely, high-context cultures, which generally include Asian Americans, Native Americans, and African Americans, consider words as only part of the message and rely heavily on nonverbal messaging and context. High-context cultures tend to prefer less eye contact. In the more general counseling experience, most clients prefer more eye contact when the counselor is speaking, and less when they are speaking (Sommers-Flanagan & Sommers-Flanagan, 2015).

9. D: Focusing on helping him cope with his strong feelings would be most helpful to the client at this stage of the therapeutic relationship. Supporting the client in taking responsibility might make the client think that you are accusing him of being wrong about his interpretation of the situation. Supporting the client in understanding his feelings might be helpful; however, it does not encourage the client to manage his strong emotions, which are often the root of his negative behavior. Empathy can be a difficult skill for someone diagnosed with ASD to conquer and therefore may not best support the client in managing his strong emotions regarding the situation.

10. D: Prompting the client to calm down when you see that he is visibly upset, but before he throws the toy, is the most helpful intervention because it addresses the client's difficulty with frustration management. Although social skills are helpful for individuals who have autism, the client was being very rigid in his thinking and needed to calm down prior to using appropriate social skills. Prompting the client to play with something else or separating the client from his brother would be avoiding dealing with the client's difficulties with frustration management.

11. D: Working in the community provides opportunities for situations like this. You are not able to tell anyone other than the client (or who you have a release of information to talk to) why you are present and who you are working with. It is most appropriate to redirect the uncle to the client's parents because the client is a minor and he may not be able to appropriately choose whether to reveal who you are. Telling the uncle that you are there as a friend of the family is not true and would not assist in developing trust with the client's uncle if you end up having to coordinate services with him also. Telling the uncle that you are the nephew's counselor would breach confidentiality, as would telling him that you are a counselor but cannot say who you are working with.

12. A: The client struggles with social skills; therefore, eye contact would likely not always be present or appropriate. The client does not appear to struggle with orientation or hygiene, although these may be factors for other individuals who have autism. Memory is not affected because the client does not have intellectual impairment.

13. C: You compiled goals for the client in the first session based on the ASD diagnosis, and you identified the client's difficulty with imaginative play. This barrier would make understanding that others have different ways of playing difficult for the client and would be the least appropriate intervention in this scenario. Deep breathing, progressive muscle relaxation, and other anger management skills would be helpful for this client because, although he will have trouble identifying with others, he can learn to manage his own strong emotions.

Case Study 2

1. C: Major depressive disorder is not indicated as a possible differential diagnosis for this client, although depression and anxiety often present together. Generalized anxiety disorder and other anxiety disorders should be assessed because the client might be having panic attacks that are based on underlying anxiety that she is experiencing. Panic disorder is characterized by unexpected panic attacks; therefore, it would be helpful to determine if the attacks are related to other anxious thoughts and cognitive processes or if they occur on their own.

2. B: Each university has a department that advocates and provides accommodations for individuals who have disabilities, including mental health conditions. Because the client is experiencing panic attacks that are affecting her academic performance, this might be an appropriate opportunity to advocate for the client's needs. The client is having trouble with attendance and attending class on time, and this would be the most important area to advocate for leniency. The client does not need to have deadlines extended because as far as you know, she is meeting the deadlines for her assignments. The department of disabilities will coordinate with her teachers; therefore, you do not need to meet with each one.

3. C: A panic attack is a triggered fight-or-flight response, and this response takes time to reduce when triggered. Reducing the frequency and intensity of panic attacks is a longer-term goal because some psychoeducation and practice with coping skills need to occur first. At this point, the client would be prepared to learn and implement coping skills and cognitive reframing. It would also be helpful for the client to begin processing the thoughts, feelings, and experiences related to her relationship with her parents.

4. C: Mindfulness is the experience of focusing only on present thoughts and feelings and learning to accept the current situation. This can be helpful in simplifying a seemingly overwhelming situation by focusing on simply existing in the moment. Some techniques to use in mindfulness include coloring or drawing, deep breathing, and body scanning. Coloring or drawing focuses the client's mind on a singular activity and helps to focus on the present. Deep breathing and body scanning focus on bodily functions and support calming the body and focusing the mind. Cognitive reframing may cause more distress because it involves working through thoughts instead of accepting a situation and focusing on the present. Cognitive reframing can be very helpful for anxiety, but when cognitive functioning is impaired by anxiety, it can be more helpful to focus the body and mind on the present.

5. A: Validating the client's choice to be in therapy and instilling hope that you believe that you can improve things are parts of the closing phase of the intake session according to Shea's model. Stating that you can help is part of closing, but coupling this with recommending interventions is part of the body of the intake session. Providing psychoeducation on the diagnosis is also part of the body of the intake session. The termination phase of the intake session is when you say goodbye to the client for that current session.

6. B: Overusing mirroring with your posture and reflection can present as unnatural or manipulative to clients (Sommers-Flanagan & Sommers-Flanagan, 2015) and would therefore be considered a negative attending behavior. Leaning forward, using hand gestures, and turning your body about 30 degrees in relation to the client are typically not a negative experience for the client unless they are excessive. Overturning your body (past 45 degrees), can be considered a negative attending behavior (Sommers-Flanagan & Sommers-Flanagan, 2015).

7. D: Radical acceptance is a DBT technique that does help with anxiety because it is about seeing the world how it is and accepting your reality, but it is not a CBT technique. Although acknowledging that a panic attack is occurring is helpful, it takes away the individual's power to change her situation if she simply accepts it. Thought stopping and reframing are helpful cognitive techniques to manage the spiraling anxious thoughts that build into panic attacks. Progressive muscle relaxation is a helpful technique to use in the moment to calm her body down physically and to calm her mind.

8. B: It is most ethical and appropriate to continue your session as scheduled, while maintaining awareness of how your personal life is affecting the counseling session because you want to support the client and prevent as much personal impact as possible. Rescheduling may be appropriate if the impact of your personal life is unavoidable; however, it is your responsibility as a therapist to ensure that you are minimizing your own personal life's impact on the client. Occasionally, you may need to directly address emotions or thoughts that you are having during sessions; however, this topic may distract from the client and reduce their confidence in your focus this session. You want to be consistent and be on time to respect your client's time and to show your investment in the client.

9. D: According to ACA ethical guidelines, dating a former client and/or someone related to that client cannot be considered until at least 5 years have passed since terminating the counseling relationship; therefore, you cannot date this individual. In a case in which 5 years had already passed, it is also necessary to provide supporting documentation that this would not be an exploitative relationship.

10. D: Evaluating the effectiveness of therapy should have occurred throughout the entirety of the counseling services; therefore, it is not a primary focus of termination. At the end of services, you want to focus on what the client has achieved and not on what you have done as a counselor. The termination session focuses on ending the relationship, encouraging the client to continue to use the learned skills without you, and helping the client to realize what has been accomplished.

11. D: Political affiliations should not affect the counseling process. You must support the client's values and beliefs even when trying to reframe what you perceive as illogical thoughts. A failed connection due to personality differences is a valid reason for referral if a connection cannot be made. Personality differences are important to consider because the therapeutic relationship relies on a real interpersonal connection between two people. If the client's needs are outside of your competency, or if the issue at hand is a medical issue or would benefit more from psychiatric intervention, then a referral is also appropriate.

12. A: There is nothing ethically wrong with working with a past client again, unless you think their current needs are outside of your scope of practice. Should symptoms worsen, your counseling would likely be very helpful for the client due to your already established rapport and familiarity with her issues. That said, it is important to encourage a client upon termination to recall the skills that were learned during your sessions as a means of preparing her for functioning and dealing with her symptoms independently. For that reason, the most appropriate response would be to first encourage her to use the learned coping skills should symptoms return, but to also reassure her that she will have access to you should those skills be insufficient. Bias is not a concern when a former client returns to counseling; rather, it would be an issue to consider should that former client request your counsel in the context of a family or a relationship, in which case you would have bias toward her over the rest of the group members.

13. A: Determining the reason for the cancellations is most important because this can open up a dialogue for getting back on track in the counseling relationship. It may be helpful to cancel future sessions if the client will receive cancellation fees, but this does not get to the bottom of what is happening with the client. It can also be helpful to encourage the client to trust the process, but this does not open up dialogue about what they are experiencing. If the client would like a referral, you should support them. However, it is more helpful to process what is causing the cancellations because it may be related to why the client is in treatment, and if unresolved, they may continue to have this issue with the next therapist.

Case Study 3

1. D: Depressive episodes are not a symptom of borderline personality disorder. There is a long list of diagnostic criteria for borderline personality disorder, five of which must be present for diagnosis. One category of criteria for borderline personality disorder, according to the DSM-5, is impulsive behavior, which includes binge eating in addition to excessive spending, inappropriate sexual relations, substance abuse, and dangerous driving. Intense anger and suicidal ideation are additional elements in the list of diagnostic criteria for borderline personality disorder.

2. C: Alcohol use disorder and other substance use disorders are important to consider for these clients with suspected borderline personality disorder. Although the symptoms that these individuals experience may be due to the substance use that is common in individuals with borderline personality disorder, alcohol use disorder must first be ruled out as the primary cause of the individual's symptoms. Reactive attachment disorder has similar symptoms but is typically a childhood disorder and would not be considered for an adult. Although conduct disorder does have behavioral or relational issues, it would not be considered a differential diagnosis. PTSD is not a differential diagnosis for borderline personality disorder.

3. A: The first step will be assisting the clients with acknowledging that they have borderline personality disorder and understanding how it affects their life because this diagnosis can be difficult for an individual to accept. Improving relationship quality, reducing urges to self-harm, and improving communication will likely take more than a month to initiate and achieve. These goals will require you to first establish a secure relationship with the group, in order for them to feel comfortable enough to explore the required complexities of their condition and its impact on relationships and feelings toward themselves.

4. B: Using dyads (breaking away into groups of two to discuss prompted topics) can be helpful in this scenario because they provide the client an opportunity to speak with a peer, a context that may be more comfortable to hesitant group members than speaking to the therapist, whom they are yet to trust. Processing with the client alone may take up valuable group time, and processing with all clients about resistance might align them against the group process. Psychoeducation about groups might be helpful; however, this happened already during the start of the intake session and was not beneficial in preventing resistance for client 3.

5. B: Because this is a group therapy session, it will not be possible to sit directly in front of each client, although that is usually a helpful way of making clients feel comfortable. You must ensure that everyone who could potentially enter your office, from clients to support staff, knows that if your door is closed, they should not enter. Allowing clients to choose the location of their seat and the type of seat provides them with a sense of comfort and control during the counseling session, while you as the counselor can still maintain some control by selecting the types of seating arrangements available. You should also make the effort to minimize distractions in the counseling setting by controlling interruptions by phones (requesting that all cell phones be placed on silent mode and considering removing or silencing any office telephones).

6. A: Using the client's motivation and focusing on what they want to work on may help in building rapport and would be using motivational interviewing techniques. Reframing thoughts uses CBT techniques. Focusing on addressing escape behaviors would be an example of a behavior therapy technique. Discussing birth order is related to Adlerian therapy.

7. D: This could be an instance of triangulation, in which client 3 is using deflection to client 2's behavior to ease client 3's stress in the session. For this reason, exploring why client 2's behavior is of concern to client 3 is the most client-centered and important focus to begin with. It might be good to keep this report in mind because it may be brought up during a group session or client 2's individual session, but you also do not know the validity of the statement unless client 2 self-reports. It is important to make sure that you do not let this information bias you, but this would not be the most pressing factor. Sharing information from your session with client 3 with client 2 would be a breach of confidentiality. Confidentiality is an important aspect to consider about DBT groups because you also provide individual therapy and need to ensure that you do not share information revealed in individual sessions in the group setting.

8. D: The use of the word *imagine* and attempting to connect with the client's situation would best demonstrate empathy. Empathy is focused on connecting and relating to the emotions expressed by the client and demonstrating your understanding to the client. Expressing sorrow with the client demonstrates an expression of sympathy because it is a reaction to someone else's distress. The response stating that it sounds like talking about the topic is difficult is an example of paraphrasing because it identifies the client's feeling and restates it. The statement stating that it sounds like the client did not feel much of a connection with his parents and acknowledging that it must be hard to talk about this topic is an example of summarization because it identifies the major elements of what was shared by the client.

9. D: Systematic desensitization is an intervention that uses aspects of CBT and applied behavioral analysis; it is not a DBT technique. Systematic desensitization focuses on progressive exposure to greater anxiety-inducing stimuli coupled with relaxation techniques. Mindfulness, emotional regulation, distress tolerance, and interpersonal effectiveness are the four focuses of DBT in improving life skills. Mindfulness focuses on becoming more aware of oneself and being present in the moment. Emotional regulation focuses on identifying, labeling, and addressing certain emotions. Distress tolerance focuses on experiencing strong emotions and not reacting impulsively or destructively.

10. C: Active listening, although helpful, is not proactive in helping members participate more when they feel like they cannot get space to speak. Dyads and rounds (enlisting a question to the group and then providing every group member the opportunity to answer) provide an individual with an unobstructed opportunity to speak and participate. Cutting off can be helpful in this situation because cutting off members that are dominating conversation and redirecting questions to client 4 can help her feel that she has an opportunity to speak.

11. D: Thought stopping is a CBT technique that is focused on stopping unhelpful thoughts before they affect functioning. TIPP (temperature, intense exercise, paced breathing, and paired muscle relaxation) is a method that helps support management of the physical symptoms of distress, therefore building distress tolerance. A pros and cons list supports the decision-making process and is part of building distress tolerance in DBT. The ability to self-soothe is also important in building distress tolerance in DBT because it involves coping with present emotions and feelings.

12. B: When dealing with rescuing in the group setting, you want to encourage members to experience the emotion that they are feeling. It would be most helpful to encourage client 5 to allow client 1 to experience his pain because he has not been participating as openly in the group process, and this demonstrates a breakthrough. If client 1 had engaged more prior to display of emotions, it may be helpful to allow client 5 to ease his pain, but currently you want client 1 to experience his feelings. Engaging with immediacy and providing coping skills can be helpful, but in this case, prioritizing the client's experience of his feelings is essential because he is just starting to participate meaningfully.

13. A: Antisocial personality disorder is defined by behavior that violates or disregards the rights of others. Argumentative, defiant, and irritable behaviors characterize oppositional defiance disorder, which is defined by persistent opposition to authority figures. Grandiosity, a need for admiration, and lack of empathy characterize narcissistic personality disorder. Severe introversion is not specific to antisocial personality disorder and would likely need further assessment to determine its cause.

Case Study 4

1. A: Autonomy is a core counseling value and is more difficult to maintain in couples counseling because there are two individuals that are both due their right to autonomy. Both individuals have varying needs, and you must balance focusing on the collective needs with focusing on the individual needs. Dual relationships, extensions of the counseling boundaries, and professional competency are factors that are less influenced by the dynamic of couples counseling.

2. C: Stabilizing the relationship is the most important goal at this point in the therapeutic relationship. It is important to determine each individual's commitment to therapy and their goals for the therapy process. This could also be an opportunity to set rules or guidelines so that certain topics are only discussed in counseling sessions, allowing the sessions to be guided and managed more effectively. Although improving communication is important, this goal will take some time because the couple has likely not been communicating wants and needs well, which may have led to the affair. It will also be helpful to focus on how the couple got to this point because this can open up conversations about deficits and needs that the couple has, but the relationship must be stabilized first. Exploring thoughts and feelings about the situation is very important and is likely a short-term goal, but making sure the couple is committed to the process and identifying their goals (to include whether the couple hopes to remain together or separate) is more pressing. Otherwise, therapy will not be productive.

3. B: You can release information to the court if the court provides an official subpoena for records. This is a situation in which you can release information without any ethical conflicts because it is a legal requirement. The husband's lawyer may be his legal representative, but you do not have written consent from the wife to release records. The wife's lawyer can request that you appear in court, but you still would not have the husband's consent to do so. Although both individuals are the identified client, you can withhold records if it causes potential harm to the other client. In this case, harm may be likely if information is released to one of the individual clients because it may affect the couple's relationships with their children. For that reason, ethically, it would not be sound judgment to release the requested records to the individuals at this time.

4. B: The Gottman Relationship Checkup assesses several areas in a relationship including conflict resolution, finances, housework, parenting, and more. This would be helpful in identifying areas that led to the affair because the relationship was likely experiencing difficulties prior to this culminating point. The Relationship Assessment Tool assesses intimate partner violence, which is not indicated for assessment at this time. The Family APGAR assessment reviews family relational aspects and would not be appropriate for the issues that this couple is experiencing. The Love Language Quiz identifies how each partner most feels and expresses love, but it is not an evidence-based theory to use during the assessment process.

5. A: According to Dr. John Gottman's four negative behaviors, or the "Four Horsemen of the Apocalypse," there are four characteristics of communication within a couple that increase the risk for divorce: stonewalling, contempt, criticism, and defensiveness. The most effective way to manage stonewalling, according to Gottman, is for the client to express that he is overwhelmed and to request a break. Walking away without saying anything would reinforce the stonewalling and would likely escalate the situation. A discussion with the couple or encouragement in coping with strong emotions together may lead to further escalation due to the gravity and rawness of the husband's emotions and would not support him in managing these strong emotions.

6. B: The Gottman Method encourages maintaining more positive than negative interactions by focusing on engaging in small acts of love often to counterbalance negative interactions. Taking breaks during conflict and regulating what you say is important, but these actions do not reflect the Gottman Method of improving positive interactions. Focusing on friendship is helpful, but this comes from engaging in positive interactions often. Communicating and dealing with conflict as it happens prevent the exacerbation of conflicts but are not the focus of the Gottman Method.

7. A: The downward arrow technique uses the client's own statements to follow their thought process to its roots, which usually reveals the underlying cause of why the original thought is hurtful. The client's original thought progressed from feeling that his wife is not attracted to him to fears that they will have a miserable marriage. Identifying this underlying fear can be helpful in targeting the deeper feelings that should be of focus during therapy. Radical acceptance is not a CBT technique and focuses on accepting the situation as it is. This may be helpful in accepting that the affair did indeed happen so that they can make a decision to either move forward together or separately. Guided discovery is a CBT technique that reflects on thoughts and feelings to discover the client's thought process. Although this situation was about discovering the client's thought process, the downward arrow technique is the specific method for how this discovery was completed. Cognitive challenging is a technique that focuses on challenging irrational or illogical beliefs or thoughts.

8. A: Improving conflict resolution skills is not currently indicated because you do not have indications that the clients are having difficulty managing conflict in the general sense. Creating a safe environment for the wife to express feelings is important because she feels like she cannot do so, demonstrated by her private expression to you outside of the session. Although the wife caused harm to her husband, her feelings and thoughts matter because the success of the couple requires both individuals to be able to communicate freely. Increasing positive interactions is a small step toward building a more positive relationship overall and can lead to rebuilding trust as both individuals begin to feel united again in their relationship. Increasing empathy skills is important because it helps each individual see the other's point of view, which creates a space for trust, understanding, and possible forgiveness.

9. C: Narrative couples therapy involves having each individual write a narrative of their own story and then guiding them to rewrite the story from a new, more positive, perspective. This process assists the couple with externalizing the problem and also with understanding that there are two sides to a conflict, which helps individuals take responsibility for their own part. By then rewriting the story, the couple is given the opportunity to rework how they will reflect on their past as they move into the future, ideally seeing their relationship more positively. Reading specific therapeutic books related to the problem areas would fall under bibliotherapy. Writing a story together and telling their story as a narrator are not defined clinical interventions specific to narrative therapy.

10. D: Supporting the husband in using coping skills is the least helpful technique in this situation because the husband needs to feel safe expressing his raw emotions in the manner that comes most naturally to him. Otherwise, repression of these feelings may occur. Muting those feelings with trained coping skills detracts from an important element of processing because the husband and wife both need to experience their emotions surrounding their situation to better understand and express their viewpoints. Immediacy would be helpful because it involves directly addressing the presenting emotions and behavior. Allowing space for the husband to experience his emotions is helpful for the husband (as a releasing process) and also for the wife (to allow her to actively experience how her spouse is feeling). Redirecting to the wife may also be helpful because this may provide her with appropriate tools for responding to her husband's emotions in a way that makes him feel supported and less isolated.

11. B: By assuming that her husband is not interested in her based on a failed attempt at a sexual interaction, the wife is jumping to conclusions in making a generalization based on a single situation. Catastrophizing is when a situation is blown out of proportion based on what occurred, and a conclusion is anticipated to be the worst possible outcome. Emotional reasoning is when an individual feels a certain way and assumes that their feelings are solely emotional and without rational justification. "Should" statements involve assuming that things should be a certain way and, when they are not, feeling a sense of distress.

12. A: The individuals in this couple are experiencing a lack of feeling validation and interest from their partner. Engaging in loving acts would most likely address these deficiencies most effectively. Although engaging in sexual intercourse may lead to validation, this was not the main concern expressed during this session. The wife focusing on guaranteeing that the husband has time to fish displays empathy and support for the husband, but it does not improve their issues with validation and connection. The couple needs to continue working on conflict resolution; however, feelings of connectedness are the couple's main focus in this session.

13. C: Despite providing coaching, the intern continues the problem behaviors, which has resulted in several clients aborting their sessions. It is apparent, at this point, that the intern is not willing to make changes and is actively harming clients, demonstrated by the client absences. For this reason, termination of the supervisor/intern relationship should be initiated (and not simply considered). If the intern is just starting to demonstrate unethical behavior, providing coaching and considering termination are appropriate actions, but these steps have already been taken. Observing a session would not be helpful because the intern likely would not engage in the problem behaviors during the session that you are watching. Furthermore, observation does not prioritize the best interest of the clients because the intern continues to engage in behavior that is harmful to them.

Case Study 5

1. D: Acute stress disorder would not be an indicated differential diagnosis; therefore, the Acute Stress Disorder Scale is not indicated here. Although it may be considered upon initial diagnosis, the client has experienced trauma symptoms over her lifetime. Acute stress disorder would not be diagnosed outside the timeframe of 3 to 30 days following the trauma exposure. Adjustment disorder would be appropriate to assess for because the client recently had some major life changes; however, the disturbances are likely a result of continuous exposure to trauma. Anxiety disorders should also be considered because PTSD has some symptoms that involve anxiety and panic. ADHD, though unlikely, could explain concentration issues and other symptoms that may appear in depression and PTSD.

2. C: The most important thing when treatment planning is to support the client's goals and objectives. Although insomnia and trauma responses are important observations as presenting symptoms, the client expressed the desire to make friends, which would be an appropriate focus in therapy because it likely would include treating most of the client's symptoms in order to reach this goal. The client's housing needs are also important to therapy and an indicated desire by the client, but this would be outside the scope of the counselor and would require either a referral for support or support from elsewhere within the government agency.

3. D: The number of criteria met that is over the minimum criteria for a diagnosis of depression is how a counselor specifies the severity of the depression as mild, moderate, or severe. This client is diagnosed with moderate depression, which is defined as being in between mild and severe depression (in which mild depression meets an amount of criteria just over the minimum requirements and severe depression meets an amount of criteria significantly over the minimum requirements). Suicidal ideation does denote the severity of the depression, but it does not affect the specifier other than being another criterion that is counted. The level of depressed mood is not measured when considering depression other than the state of being in a depressed mood more often than not. The effect of depression on functioning is an important criterion to consider and is also a criterion for the diagnosis of major depressive disorder.

4. D: Although depression can cause suicidal ideation, it has been shown that depression alone is often not the factor that leads to suicide attempts. Rather, a combination of other issues has been proven to correlate with suicidal ideation, including a history of trauma, hopelessness, anxiety, panic attacks, substance use, and self-harm (Sommers-Flanagan & Sommers Flanagan, 2015). Substance use, recklessness, and hopelessness can all attribute to a general disturbance in the client's ability to make sound decisions, leading to possible suicide attempts.

5. A: Creating a genogram could be very helpful with this client because it examines relationships with family members and is a visual representation of these relationships including the psychological factors that affect the family and the client. This can be helpful in understanding where this client came from and how it shaped her current functioning. Creating a genogram can also help open up a conversation regarding her history. The Clinician-Administered PTSD Scale for DSM-5 might be helpful in understanding the client's level of PTSD symptomatology, but it would not give insight into the client's relationship patterns. The Relationship Assessment Scale identifies general satisfaction levels in a current relationship and would not be helpful for this client. The Adult Attachment Interview might be helpful in understanding the client's attachment with her parents, but the genogram would provide a more global understanding of the client's family history and the client's relationships with others in her family.

6. B: Focusing on the current situation, in which the roommate has not done anything other than disrespect boundaries, and seeing how it is different from past events is the most helpful cognitive reframe. This focuses on the reality and helps the client refrain from blowing it out of proportion. Although focusing on enforcing boundaries is helpful, it is not a cognitive reframe. Identifying that it is a possibility that the roommate may sexually assault her is not helpful because this reinforces fear and irrational thinking. Identifying that the client's thoughts are not reality is important, but this does not focus on the root of the thoughts, which stem from a fear of a past situation becoming the present reality.

7. B: Providing empathy and encouraging cognitive reframing are helpful because these actions validate the client's experience, even if you do not think that it is rooted in reality, and it provides an opportunity for her to identify other ways to think about the situation. Simply validating the client's experience does not provide the client with other options about how to feel or think. Challenging beliefs does not validate the client's experience and may make the client feel unheard or that you do not think she is being rational. Encouraging reframing on its own may put pressure on the client to feel a certain way. Pairing empathy with cognitive reframing is a more holistic approach to supporting the client.

8. D: The client is experiencing the cognitive distortion of jumping to conclusions. The client is using past experiences regarding her trauma to infer that this present situation will end in the same way. Labeling is about assigning value or labels to ourselves or others. Personalization is about taking blame or responsibility for the situation and would not relate to this client's thoughts during this session. All-or-nothing, or black-or-white, thinking implies that a situation is either one way or the complete opposite. This would not apply because the client is assuming results based on prior experiences rather than assigning an all-or-nothing quality to the situation.

9. A: Exposure therapy, when completed over an appropriate period of time with gradually more difficult exposures, can be effective in treating the avoidance-related symptoms of PTSD. Although it makes sense that an individual would want to avoid stimuli that trigger strong emotions, restaurants and stores are not actual threats to the client, and her avoidance of these settings is inhibiting her ability to live her life. Through gradual exposure, the client can see that she is safe in those environments and does not need to avoid them. DBT and CBT are each therapy modalities that have cognitive and behavioral aspects that might benefit treatment of PTSD, but they do not address the avoidance behavior adequately on their own. Integrative therapy is the blending of different therapy techniques for a holistic approach to treatment; however, this would not be as effective in treating avoidance behaviors.

10. A: The transtheoretical model of change proposes six stages of change: precontemplation, contemplation, preparation, action, maintenance, and termination. This client is in the preparation stage of change because she understands her problem and has a plan in place to address it. The client is not currently taking actions to make changes; therefore, she is not in the action phase of change. The precontemplation phase occurs prior to the client identifying the problem when the client may not have any intention of addressing her behavior. The contemplation phase involves the client knowing that there is a problem but not yet having a plan for action.

11. C: Reaching out to an emergency contact after one missed session is not by itself a sufficient justification for disclosure because you are unsure if the client is at imminent risk of harm. You may disclose information to the insurance company because they are a payor. You can also break confidentiality if the client is at risk of harming themselves or others. Even when the client is deceased, you must maintain confidentiality to the level requested by the client.

12. A: Validating your client's emotions and engaging in coping skills is the most appropriate response because the client is in the preparation stage of change and knows what the problem is but is not able to make changes yet. Validating emotions and helping the client cope in the moment deals with the client's presenting emotions. Challenging cognitive distortions would be part of the action stage, and the client is not ready to engage in this step yet. Simply empathizing with the client may build rapport but will not help the client develop skills to manage strong emotions. Validating the client's emotions and beliefs based on her past experiences may reinforce her labeling of herself and may also demonstrate that you think the client is incapable of changing her future experiences.

13. C: Identifying the match in value between the bartered items or services is not an ethical consideration related to bartering. The ACA Code of Ethics identifies that the important factors to ensure as they relate to bartering include that exploitation or harm does not occur as part of bartering, that the client initiates bartering and not the therapist, and the consideration of whether it is common practice in the community to trade goods or services.

Case Study 6

1. D: Although anorexia is a mental health disorder, it is also a medical diagnosis, and medical considerations need to be part of the client's treatment. The client should have regular appointments with her PCP to monitor her health. Inpatient treatment is not indicated at this time based on the information provided and because you specialize in eating disorders and are qualified to counsel this patient right now. A dentist referral should be considered because purging and poor nutrition affect tooth health. Psychiatrist-prescribed medication can be helpful in managing mood and anxiety related to anorexia. A nutritionist can be helpful for the client in identifying healthier eating habits and learning more about nutrition's effects on the body.

2. B: This approach to building rapport is called unconditional positive regard. This is used to demonstrate to the client that you accept her as she is and are genuinely interested in understanding what she is experiencing. Congruence is about being a genuine honest person and matching your external expressions to how you internally feel. It is not related to the concept of recognizing the client as the expert of herself. Congruence provides the client with the insight that the therapist is also a human and requires the management of counselor and client boundaries because self-disclosure and being openly emotional may cause the client to want to support the counselor. Mutuality involves sharing decision making, treatment planning, and power, while the therapist and client are both learning as they go. The identification and internalization process is about modeling behaviors or skills and internalizing them.

3. A: Appropriate homework for this client after her first session would be to encourage her to complete a daily food log so you can have baseline data on her current eating habits. Providing psychoeducation is helpful, but a book might be too much for a client just starting therapy, and you are also still in the information-gathering phase. Behavioral experiments such as trying triggering foods and creating a hierarchy are both activities that the therapist needs to guide to ensure that no harm is caused; therefore, these interventions are not appropriate for homework.

4. A: Trauma is most indicated as a focus for assessment because the client's mother is deceased and the manner of her passing is directly connected to the client's thought process surrounding her eating patterns. Anxious and depressive symptoms might be present, but they are not the most debilitating symptoms. The client's relationship quality is also important to consider; however, the client's trauma regarding her mother appears to be the most likely root to some of her eating disorder symptoms and triggers and should therefore be considered and investigated first.

5. C: Dependent personality disorder is characterized by feeling incapable of caring for or making decisions for oneself and is not a differential diagnosis for anorexia nervosa. Bulimia nervosa is similar to anorexia nervosa because it involves compensatory eating or exercise behavior; however, it is often accompanied by a more normal weight due to binges. Social anxiety disorder may also be a differential diagnosis if the client's extreme eating habits result from fear with regard to the judgment of being watched while eating. Hyperthyroidism can be an undiagnosed cause of excessive weight loss. Pathophysiologic causes must always be ruled out if they are a suspected cause of a symptom.

6. C: It is most important to first consider your own motives for any personal reaction, similar to self-disclosure, because you want to make sure that you are responding for the client's benefit and not for your own management of emotional response or emotional needs. Although handshakes are generally acceptable, clients may also respond well to other types of physical touch and may benefit from a comforting hand on the shoulder. Sexual orientation and the client's identified gender are important considerations; however, your motives are the first filter in assessing the benefits of physical touch. Although physical touch is a typical and accepted human response, you should be careful about the impacts of this response.

7. A: While identifying the reality of becoming overweight and its possible consequences may carry elements of truth, there is a balance that needs to be found when reframing this client's cognition. The thought that she could become overweight and suffer the consequences (her husband's unhappiness and her own death), but that she can do something to keep that from happening may accept a reality, but it also encourages the unhealthy behavior that the client already engages in. In this situation, identifying that her body is not letting her down and that her worth is not defined by weight is a healthier balance in thinking.

8. C: This cognitive distortion is considered emotional reasoning, which is defined as "I feel; therefore, it must be true." Personalization is when the client assumes that she is responsible for what happened and would not define the present cognitive distortion. This cognitive distortion is also not an example of "always being right" because the client is not expressing that the possibility that she is wrong is unacceptable. Overgeneralization is when the client assumes a generalized rule from a singular experience. Overgeneralization may explain why she feels like she is going to die because her mother did, but it does not explain why she feels being overweight means that she has no worth.

9. D: The only medication with evidence-based proof of effectiveness in treating anorexia nervosa is olanzapine, a second-generation antipsychotic that has proven to be effective in the case of severe illness associated with drastic weight loss in anorexia. Olanzapine has shown the ability to aid in weight gain in this scenario. Antidepressants such as SSRIs and tricyclic antidepressants have not shown evidence of improving the negative behaviors associated with anorexia or in improving negative thoughts and distorted self-image, although antidepressants, specifically fluoxetine, have been recommended and are proven effective in the treatment of bulimia nervosa. Benzodiazepines slow down the information traveling between the brain and body and are not an effective treatment of anorexia nervosa.

10. B: As your first response, it would be most helpful to support the client in having an effective conversation with her husband regarding her health and progress. If this is unhelpful, providing a referral for couples counseling might be the next best course of action. You would not invite the husband to sessions because you are the client's individual therapist and would therefore not be an appropriate fit as the couple's therapist due to the potential for bias. It can be helpful to support the client in coping with her husband's level of frustration, but this is not the most helpful course of action because it implies acceptance of a situation that is potentially harmful to her progress.

11. B: It is not always realistic to expect all symptoms to be abated. When minimal symptoms are present and the client is able to manage them and maintain progress, termination is appropriate. Although no symptoms being present is the ideal, this may never be attainable in some clients; therefore, it is appropriate to terminate when the client is able to be autonomous and manage her symptoms by herself. The client having nothing to talk about is not ideal for termination because this may indicate that she is not reporting or not being forthcoming with what she is experiencing. The client's report regarding eating habits and a plan for couples counseling is good progress, but it does not focus on the client's autonomy regarding her ability to manage symptoms on her own. Symptoms may be present long after therapy, but one of the most important aspects of counseling is that the client is able to self-regulate and manage what life sends to her.

12. B: The client has achieved treatment goals and now social support systems are the most appropriate intervention for maintenance; therefore, support groups would be beneficial by connecting her to others who are experiencing similar struggles. Providing results of screenings does not empower the client to use social support systems, but it may show her that she has been successful and has made progress. You should be careful in showing pride in her success, so that it is clear you are proud of her success, not your own skill as a counselor. It is helpful to let the client know that she should not feel shame in restarting counseling if she needs to, but this does not show her that she has made progress or that you believe that she can manage her emotions on her own.

13. A: Having different values is not a reason to terminate counseling because you must be able to provide counseling to others with different views and maintain objectivity. Rather, seeking counseling in the situation of different values is the appropriate consideration. When the client no longer needs counseling, termination is appropriate to consider because you are providing a service that is not needed. When the client cannot pay the agreed-upon fees, it is also appropriate to consider termination. If the counselor is at risk of harm by the client or by relationships that the client has, then termination is necessary.

Case Study 7

1. A: ADHD is a mental health diagnosis, but it is also a medical diagnosis because it is a developmental disorder. You need to receive records from the PCP and historical documentation regarding symptomology to confirm this diagnosis. Do not attempt to diagnose ADHD on your own. You can also give a provisional diagnosis while you work through narrowing down the client's diagnosis. This is a difficult diagnosis to confirm on your own, especially through telehealth sessions, and you should collaborate with other medical/mental health professionals who have seen this client in person.

2. B: Identifying the current ADHD behaviors that cause the most difficulty for the client is the most important first step in this client's therapy, followed by determining the impact of symptoms on functioning. Encouraging the participation of the client's girlfriend may provide insight into the client's functioning and may also provide a social support for the client; however, relationship issues were not indicated in the first session. Organization skills and cognitive reframing are important parts of therapy for treatment of ADHD; however, they are not the first step. Psychoeducation on reframing and organization must be prioritized as well, but you need to identify the behaviors that cause the most difficulty to begin working on these skills.

3. D: According to a meta-analysis of ADHD questionnaires and assessment tools performed in 2016, the Conners Abbreviated Symptom Questionnaire is the most effective tool for screening for ADHD due to its ability to assess for positive and negative symptoms. This tool will be the most helpful because it probes functioning in many areas including work, home, school, and social functioning with ADHD. The Vanderbilt ADHD Diagnostic Rating Scale would not be appropriate for this patient because it assesses ages 6 through 12 for ADHD. The Vineland Adaptive Behavior Scales would also be inappropriate for this client because it is used for people ages 3 through 21. Although an organizational assessment may be helpful, it is not an approved means of diagnosing ADHD.

4. D: Considering the client's presenting problems, which include the identification of often feeling unhappy, assessing for major depressive disorders is appropriate because they can co-occur with

ADHD. Anxiety may be present surrounding completing tasks; however, this anxiety is likely related to ADHD and is not indicated as a possible diagnosis. There are no reports of substance use, so this would not be considered for this client at this time.

5. D: The use of self-disclosure is a helpful therapeutic tool in demonstrating empathy and can benefit the counseling relationship when used appropriately. Self-disclosure should only occur when it would be beneficial to the therapeutic process; it should be used discriminately. Completely refraining from using self-disclosure prevents the counselor from access to a potentially helpful tool.

6. D: Training as an educator is not a prerequisite to speaking regarding areas that you specialize in as a counselor, even if it is in an educational setting. The ACA Code of Ethics states that you are within your limits as a counselor if you base your lecture on accepted literature and practices, the group knows that you are not establishing a counseling relationship with them, and your statements align with the ACA Code of Ethics.

7. A: To build momentum with new goals, it can be helpful to identify goals that are easily achievable to increase the client's confidence in goal attainment. Considering that playing guitar and writing are new goals, you would not focus on identifying slightly more difficult goals because these are new skills and rigor should start lower and slowly build. Recommending a specific interval of attempts toward the goal does not consider what the client thinks is achievable and likely would not build confidence and momentum toward a goal. Although the client came to counseling for ADHD, his symptoms of concern are likely linked to his desire to play guitar more and to start writing again. For this reason, refocusing back more explicitly and specifically on his initial ADHD difficulties at work would not be appropriate.

8. C: Orientation to person, place, time, and situation can be observed and assessed regardless of the session being provided via telehealth. Body language is a unique consideration in telehealth, and you might have more difficulty assessing the client's body language, such as hand gestures, bouncing legs, shaking hands, etc. The counselor's body language and the counseling room environment are not as important or impactful, aside from what the client sees behind you on his or her computer screen. Costs for telehealth sessions can be cheaper at times than in-person sessions. An additional cost for the counselor might be a HIPAA-compliant telehealth medium. Confidentiality remains the same in that sessions should remain confidential; however, you cannot guarantee that no one is listening in or is in the room in the client's location.

9. D: When considering depression, activities often seem like they will not be as enjoyable as they are in reality; therefore, it is important to try them anyway. When using cognitive reframing, it is important to consider the notion that if no changes are made, things will remain the same. Encouraging the client to remind himself that he may enjoy the simple process of playing guitar is not as relevant because it does not account for the client's ability to effect change. The notion that the client should wait until he is "ready to play" allows space for him to find excuses not to play if he is struggling with the impacts of depression and ADHD. Although creating a plan to complete a goal can help the client in goal achievement, it likely will not empower the client to manage his present emotions and thoughts.

10. C: Identifying goals by determining what is important to the client would likely be the most helpful next step because the client has not been prioritizing his sessions. Refocusing on what is now most important to the client might increase motivation and participation. Over the course of therapy, needs change and therapy needs to be refocused to maintain motivation and to work toward meaningful goals. Asking "why" questions often puts the client in a position in which he feels the need to justify himself and can create defensiveness, which is not helpful in processing the client's behavior. Reviewing previous treatment goals likely would not help very much because the client does not seem to be finding those goals meaningful anymore. Discussing scheduling likely would not be helpful because the client is actively scheduling other activities over the current scheduled sessions, which demonstrates that he has availability during this time but he is prioritizing other activities.

11. A: The client is not prioritizing counseling, as evidenced by his list of activities he is participating in that have interrupted his ability to attend. It would be important to focus on how to make sessions meaningful to the client by identifying goals and interventions that matter to him. You have explored depression as another diagnosis; however, there is a possibility that this is not the priority issue because interventions have not motivated the client to continue to attend his sessions. The client's organizational skills are an issue secondary to his ADHD diagnosis; however, you would still want to find a way to engage him in therapy by making it meaningful for him. Scheduling conflicts are not likely an issue because the client is finding time to attend a long list of other activities that do not seem to be impacted by scheduling conflicts.

12. A: Fidgeting is a common psychomotor activity for individuals who have ADHD and many other mental health disorders. This may be hard to assess because sessions are conducted via telehealth. Scanning and excessive eye movement are likely more related to anxiety, paranoia, and other mental health disorders, not ADHD. Posturing is not a typical symptom associated with ADHD. Pacing is typically associated with anxiety disorders, panic attacks, and at times autism spectrum disorders with repetitive behaviors.

13. B: If you determine that the client is not going to initiate contact regarding services, then reaching out several times to ensure that he knows how to reconnect with you or another therapist is an appropriate next step. This demonstrates that you have attempted to follow up with the client and that you are not abandoning him. Termination based only on whether the client is voluntary or involuntary does not matter because you want to ensure that the client has the information that he needs and that you make every effort to continue services. Continuing to attempt contact without a cutoff point does not make the best use of your time, and it does not put the responsibility on the client to decide if therapy is important enough for him to participate in. Reaching out once and waiting for a response might be missed by the client and does not demonstrate genuine attempts to support the client.

Case Study 8

1. A: The court can subpoena information if needed, and records must be provided in such cases. Therefore, it is best to gain consent from the client, if possible, so you are not sharing information against his wishes, while also explaining to the client certain limits in confidentiality that are unique to his circumstances. Limiting the amount of information provided to the court or attempting to restrict it altogether if it is best for the client is ideal because it protects your counseling relationship. The other answer options do not fulfill the counselor's needs to meet court orders and to protect the counseling relationship. Sharing all information does not allow the client to have space to speak freely with you, yet you also cannot restrict all information from the court.

2. B: Depression is not indicated based on the presenting symptoms. Although depression may co-occur with inhalant use because the use of substances may alleviate depressive symptoms, the client did not report any depression symptoms. Grief and trauma related to the client's son passing away are important areas to explore because these appear to be the triggering symptoms that led to his substance use. The client's relationship with his ex-wife would be important to explore because the client is not able to see his children as much as he wants due to his substance use. The client also wants to maintain employment, so it would be helpful to focus on barriers to maintaining employment.

3. D: Within PTSD, the criteria for trauma symptoms requires that they must last longer than 1 month following the traumatic event. Acute stress disorder has similar criteria to PTSD, but it occurs only 3 days to 1 month following the traumatic event. Poor concentration, difficulty remembering the events of the traumatic event, and irritability are all symptoms of PTSD.

4. B: A genogram would give more information regarding family dynamics, relationship quality and status, family patterns, and family substance use. Genograms are a great tool to use to understand how the client's family contributed to where he is at currently. Discussing the genogram will give a lot more information because it presents many opportunities to discuss his relationships and history. You will conduct a mental status exam each session, but this will likely not provide much information regarding behavior and is more about the client's presentation in session. A thought log would be helpful over time to understand how the client processes information and is also helpful for the client to become more aware of how thoughts, feelings, and behaviors affect his functioning, but the genogram would be more helpful in providing information and encouraging conversation regarding his behavior and his past relationships. It might be helpful to communicate with the client's ex-wife; however, she would likely be a biased party, which could complicate the counseling relationship.

5. D: The client may choose to discontinue therapy early; however, this is not a risk of the counseling process, rather, a decision on the part of the client. Therapy can make things worse initially because the client may have to discuss or confront situations, thoughts, and feelings that may cause distress. This is an expected part of the therapeutic process. The client may need to meet with multiple counselors prior to finding a match who meets his needs for building rapport and who also has the skill set needed to best support the client.

6. B: Helping the client identify that he is not where he wants to be (in terms of breaking his sobriety) and then identifying that he can start working with his counselor and sponsor to improve his situation is the most helpful reframe to his cognitive distortion. It is most helpful to be realistic with the presenting problem and to choose a path forward. Although the reframe that he may not be able to improve the relationship or visitation agreement might have some truth to it, improving these situations is important for his relationship with his children and for his own mental health; therefore, these are important to continue to focus improvement efforts on. Contacting the lawyer may be helpful for the visitation agreement, but this will not guarantee that the client is going to be okay moving forward. The client needs to improve his behavior and thought processes to maintain sobriety and therefore improve visitations for the long term. Identifying that the client broke sobriety and needs to get back on track is true, but it does not provide the next steps for improving his situation.

7. A: This is an example of emotional reasoning. The client felt guilt and shame for breaking his sobriety, and he used these emotions to justify the feeling that it would not matter if he used inhalants again. Jumping to conclusions involves either trying to predict the future or assuming others' thoughts and feelings. Magnification involves focusing on shortcomings and exaggerating their importance or effect and minimizing positive qualities and behaviors. Mental filters involve focusing solely on a shortcoming and ignoring everything else.

8. D: Insomnia is not typically associated with inhalants. Rather, inhalants generally slow down the body's movement, slow reflexes, and cause a stupor, likely leading to sleepiness. Nystagmus (uncontrollable eye movement), euphoria (feelings of great happiness or excitement), and muscle weakness are common symptoms of inhalant intoxication.

9. A: Acceptance and commitment therapy focuses on accepting present emotions and staying present in those thoughts and emotions without judgment. Accepting the situation and realizing the ability to change it is a CBT approach. The focus on human abilities and limitations is key to existential therapy. A focus on repressed emotions and experiences is a feature of psychoanalysis.

10. C: A balanced use of affirmative sounds ("mhmm," "yeah," etc.) lets the client know that you are listening to him. Be conscientious about how often you use these responses because they can be distracting, may appear as though you are rushing the client, or may appear as though you are disinterested. Silence generally does not provide the client with the feedback that you are listening to him. However, attentive silence with body language that demonstrates you are listening can allow the client the space to speak freely. Mirroring involves repeating key words or phrases that the client uses to demonstrate that you heard the important pieces of what was said. Identifying and expressing that you notice inconsistencies in verbal and nonverbal communication is important but needs to be done carefully. This demonstrates to the client that you hear him and recognize how he feels.

11. D: Termination would not be your primary concern when suspecting that this client is intoxicated. Although you may want to consider ending the current session, a discussion about termination would not be very helpful in the client's current state and it does not support his needs at the moment. It is important to consider whether continuing the session is going to cause more harm, be helpful, or do nothing for the client. You do not know what the client is like when he uses inhalants; therefore, this could be a dangerous or harmful circumstance. You do need to consider how the client will get home if he is planning on driving and is unable to drive. It is important to know state laws because you may be liable if someone gets hurt when the client is driving home. It may be appropriate to try and process what led the client to use when he left the office because you might gain further insight into his condition.

12. C: The client continues to use inhalants regularly despite counseling, and it is causing harm to his relationships and putting him and others at risk of harm. An inpatient drug rehabilitation facility might be a more appropriate level of care. A referral to another counselor would likely produce the same results because the counselor can only provide counseling twice weekly and cannot monitor or support him between sessions as well as an inpatient facility could. Psychiatric hospitalization may be helpful to stabilize the client quickly, but it would not provide the therapeutic level of support that the client needs to reestablish and maintain sobriety. Case management might be helpful; however, case management connects the client to services and supports functioning and this takes some time to set up and provide the funded services. The client needs more immediate support to keep him from causing further harm to his relationships and to decrease the risk that the client might pose to himself and others.

13. C: The client does retain rights in court-ordered therapy, and you must get a release of information to provide the probation officer with the requested notes if a subpoena is not provided. Even when a client, including a minor, does not retain rights, it is important to get the client's consent to services in order to preserve trust in the counseling relationship.

Case Study 9

1. B: Major depressive disorders often present in children and adolescents as aggression, irritability, and conduct problems; therefore, it is important to rule out depressive disorders when assessing a child that presents this way. Reactive attachment disorder involves an unstable attachment with caregivers, and it is not considered a differential diagnosis for conduct disorder. Although antisocial personality disorder and conduct disorder both involve the violation of the rights of others, a diagnosis of antisocial personality disorder requires the child to be at least 15 years of age. Autism spectrum disorders are at times characterized by behavioral dysfunction that stems from having difficulty feeling empathy, but they are not defined by an intentional violation of the rights of others.

2. B: The client is likely often in trouble with his parents, and teachers and other adults likely side with his parents when he is in trouble. It would be beneficial to your counseling relationship to show the client that you understand why he engages in these behaviors and why he might be frustrated or angry or why he may feel misunderstood. Rapport will be built over time, but coming alongside your client by helping him feel like you are on his side and that you want him to be happy and enjoy himself will be much more beneficial and more proactive. Providing enjoyable activities or playing with your client might increase rapport; however, the client is old enough to engage in cognitive therapeutic work, which might be more beneficial. Although it is important to support the parents, you are the client's therapist and you need to promote his interests and help him engage in them in a more appropriate manner.

3. A: DBT is not considered effective for treatment of conduct disorder. DBT is a modified version of CBT that was created for treatment of personality disorders, and it has also been proven effective with depression and bipolar disorder. CBT would be helpful in supporting the client in processing his thoughts more effectively in order to improve his behavior; it also has a focus on emotional regulation, which the client would benefit from. Family therapy would be appropriate to consider because the client and his family system are not functioning well as a whole and could use support in reestablishing relationships to become a more effective family system. The client could benefit from medication management for support in managing strong emotions.

4. C: The Diagnostic Interview for Children and Adolescents tests for many different DSM-5 disorders including conduct disorder. This can be helpful in ensuring that the diagnosis is accurate and that it is not a different disorder. There is also a version that can be given to the parents to validate the assessment results given to their child. The Conners Continuous Performance Test can provide supporting information to validate the conduct disorder diagnosis, but it is geared more toward impulsivity in the test-taking environment. The Child Behavior Checklist assesses for many behaviors and can support the diagnosis, but it would not specifically lead to a diagnosis of conduct disorder. The Delinquent Activities Scale does diagnose conduct disorder specifically but only for incarcerated adolescents.

5. D: The MSE examines behavior and functioning during the present session. The client's thought process (e.g., coherent, grandiose, fleeting ideas, or delusional), insight, and memory are all part of MSE testing. You assess the client's thought process throughout the session by noting his ability to communicate thoughts and feelings and to stay on topic during the session. Insight is the client's awareness of the impact of mental health on functioning. This can be assessed by noticing if the client can identify if his behavior is problematic at home and in the school setting. Memory is assessed by noting if the client is able to recall events and remember what was talked about in this and previous sessions. Diagnosis is not part of the MSE.

6. B: Your obligation as a mandated reporter is to report allegations of abuse, neglect, or exploitation of minors, regardless of whether you think they are credible or not. It is the local government agency's responsibility to assess and determine if allegations are founded. Do not wait too long after the abuse to report it for several reasons. Your state may have laws on the time frame to report (e.g., some states require that you report allegations within 24 hours of the report), and the client may in fact be at risk of further harm from his father if the allegations are true. Bringing the parents into the session can be helpful in certain circumstances, but it is important to consider if this may cause more harm to your client because the father may retaliate toward him.

7. C: Consistency and structure are important for anyone, but they are especially for someone with conduct disorder. Although a reward system may be beneficial in treating behavior related to conduct disorder, it is not an intervention that is focused on enhancing the parents' understanding of attachment and is therefore the least appropriate option in meeting that goal. In fact, reward systems can potentially strain attachment. Reading related to positive attachment would be beneficial for the parents and likely would include information on attachment-enhancing activities such as intentional one-on-one activities and consistent family time.

8. B: The family system has smaller systems within it that are created, often naturally, based on many different categories, such as gender, age, hierarchy (parent/child), function (who is responsible for what in the home), common interests, or common characteristics. These subsystems generally consist of two to three people who establish roles between them and within the system. The client is an individual and therefore would not be considered a subsystem. The parents are a hierarchical and a generational subsystem. The siblings are another subsystem based on ages/interests and likely have established certain roles that the client may feel ostracized from. The social family members are a subsystem with similar characteristics, and they are bonded over enjoying similar activities.

9. A: When the client escalates to using physical aggression, he is likely not able to engage in processing his thoughts and emotions. It may escalate the behavior further if you attempt to have a conversation with the client. Using the 5-4-3-2-1 grounding technique is helpful because it focuses on engaging the senses and it can help the client calm his body down. Using an open body posture and a calm voice supports the client in not feeling threatened. When the client's level of intensity is not matched, he is more likely to reduce the level of intensity of his emotions to match the counselor's. It can be assumed that the client's behavior is an attempt to avoid talking about a difficult topic. In behavior therapy, you would not want to allow the avoidance to occur; however, this might be related to a trauma response because it is about a physical abuse allegation. Therefore, you should strive to be understanding and sensitive about possible trauma.

10. A: The function of this client's behavior when he blames others is to escape consequences and escape possible pain from being in trouble or having to accept his own behavior. The client is not seeking attention because he is redirecting attention. The client might blame others in an attempt to maintain access to activities or items, but in the case of a client with conduct disorder, he is likely trying to avoid punishment. There is no indication that this client is looking for sensory input or cognitive stimulation.

11. C: Empathizing with the client and showing him that you are on his side and want him to live a happy life is likely going to be the most encouraging approach for this client. This also empowers the client to understand that he can play by the rules and get what he wants instead of breaking the rules, not getting what he wants, and suffering consequences. Focusing on the consequences alone does not address that you acknowledge his wants and needs and that you want to support him in meeting these needs. It may be helpful to reexamine the reward system, but the reward system is not a long-term tool and is not focused on the client's internal motivation. Although the client may continue to improve and eventually agree to make changes with different rewards, this is not a proactive strategy because it does not foster internal motivation.

12. B: "Should" statements occur when your expectations for how something should be is incongruent with what actually happened. This often incites anger because you expect someone to act a certain way, such as being kind to you, and variations on that expectation are disruptive. Personalization is when an individual thinks that they are responsible for things outside of their control, and this usually leads to the individual thinking that they can make things better even when they are likely not able to. Disqualifying the positive occurs when the client ignores all positives and focuses only on negative events. Catastrophizing is when the client sees only the worst possible outcome even when it is not the most likely outcome. Although anger may result from personalization, disqualification, and catastrophizing, these are more likely to result in disappointment, shame, anxiety, and/or negativity.

13. D: The client has agreed to certain payment expectations as outlined in the informed consent documents and is not paying as agreed. You are able to refrain from waiving the payments if you would prefer because they have been consented to. Informing the client of intentions to use a collections agency, allowing the opportunity to pay for recent sessions, and including this information in the informed consent are all important ethical considerations in this situation, according to the ACA Code of Ethics.

Case Study 10

1. A: Masturbation can relieve this client's aforementioned stress and tension, and therefore anxiety, through the release of hormones such as dopamine, endorphins, and others that improve mood and physical feelings. Those same "feel-good" hormones might also temporarily improve how the client feels about himself; however, self-esteem is not an issue that has been indicated at this time. Loneliness is not indicated in this client's case either; however, an individual who feels alone might use pornography to feel a connection to other humans. The client's behavior does seem to be compulsive, but it is not this client's most likely reason for masturbation.

2. D: The most factual statement regarding client records is with regard to making reasonable precautions in case you are suddenly unable to continue services. Even if a counseling resident is practicing under your license, you still need to obtain written consent for release of information to your resident. When a client requests records, if there is a risk of foreseeable harm, you can restrict access to some or all of the client's chart. You should keep the client's records within the bounds of the state's laws within which you practice, which is typically a certain number of years, but the length of time varies based on the state in which you are licensed. Some clients have situations that might suggest that you keep records longer such as those having court involvement or abuse/neglect allegations.

3. D: Cortisol is a stress-induced hormone that is released when the fight-or-flight response is triggered. It regulates mood as it relates to stress; it also regulates the immune system, the inflammatory response, and blood sugar levels. Cortisol is not released by the act of masturbation. Oxytocin relates more to breastfeeding and childbirth; however, it is also linked with increased feelings of bonding during sexual intercourse and even while hugging. Testosterone increases stamina during sexual intercourse and the level of arousal. Dopamine is considered a "happiness" hormone and is part of the brain's reward system that leads to increased desires for sexual intercourse in order to receive this hormonal reward. As a counselor, it is helpful to know how these hormones affect functioning because they can be a large factor in behavior and cognitions being reinforced and increasing in frequency or intensity.

4. B: The client wants to focus initially on cessation of pornography use and his unhappiness in the workplace. Exploring what the client has liked and disliked about his current and past employment is an appropriate short-term goal that can open up conversations about possibly changing the employment and identifying what matters to the client when at work. Although decreasing the frequency of masturbation may happen in the first month, you likely will only have a few sessions in this time period, and the skills necessary to manage urges to masturbate will not likely be developed at this point. Assertiveness skills training can be helpful in improving work situations; however, the client has already had several conversations with his supervisors and it does not appear that they have been open to his input thus far. The client does have a generalized anxiety diagnosis; however, he has more immediately pressing issues that he wants to work on, so you likely will not master coping skills for anxiety within the first month.

5. D: Focusing on improving self-esteem might help reduce the frequency of masturbation; however, it is not a behavioral intervention. Exercise releases chemicals in the body that improve mood and can help reduce the desire to masturbate. Spending time with family or friends can be helpful in extinguishing masturbation urges, especially if a root cause of these urges is loneliness. Blocking pornographic websites limits or delays the client's access to contributory resources for his masturbation, which can provide the client with time to use coping skills to manage the urge to masturbate.

6. D: Snapping a rubber band on the wrist can be helpful in stopping some bad habits (cursing, negative thinking, etc.); however, this often leads to avoiding dealing emotionally with what is happening and would not likely stop the client from masturbating. Conversely, reading the Bible, praying, or calling a friend are ways for this client to emotionally deal with these urges and will remind the client of his motivation to refrain from masturbating. Leaving his bedroom or going for a drive would be incompatible with masturbation and may also act as a healthy distraction.

7. C: This exemplifies overgeneralization because the client is taking his experience at the current position and applying it to his future employment opportunities. Overgeneralization does not take into account different factors such as supervising style, skills the client has, etc., and because of this, it is likely not an accurate thought pattern. Although the client's statement may have a level of fortune telling, it does not account for the use of the past experience to inform future experiences. Catastrophizing is assuming the worst possible outcome, which is not what the client is doing in this situation. Emotional reasoning assumes that "I feel incompetent; therefore, I must be incompetent," which is not what the client is doing in this case. Rather, he is taking past experiences and projecting them onto future experiences.

8. D: Although summarizing shows that you are listening, it does not necessarily actively support the client in feeling more comfortable regarding a topic. Immediacy is when you address what you are seeing in the session, when you see it. This may induce some discomfort, but it will likely lead to talking through the anxiety, shame, and guilt that the client feels when talking about this topic. Self-awareness of the counselor applies to the verbal and nonverbal reactions that the counselor portrays while the client opens up about his struggles with masturbation. The counselor should maintain self-awareness when reacting to the client on this topic so as to create a safe environment of openness and to deepen therapeutic rapport. Although normalizing would likely not be helpful for the client in the sense of normalizing masturbation (because this is a religious and, therefore, internal struggle for him), it might be helpful to normalize the client's humanity as an imperfect being who struggles with certain behaviors.

9. B: Mood is the most likely element of the mental status exam to be affected during this client's sessions because he has verbalized feelings of anxiety, guilt, and shame in discussing his struggles, all of which may impact his mood. Eye contact may have been difficult during the early sessions for this client because he was still in the process of building rapport; however, this is your fourth session and the client is less likely to be experiencing social anxiety and discomfort with the therapeutic relationship. Suicidality is not a reported or observed concern due to the client's diagnoses or reports. Orientation does not appear to be affected because the client is alert and oriented to time, location, self, and situation.

10. B: The best reframe in this case of all-or-nothing thinking is the client acknowledging that he did not meet his goal but that he has power over the rest of his day to make changes. This reframe helps the client see that one event in his day does not have to define the whole day. Acknowledging his humanity is helpful, but it does not address the client's all-or-nothing thinking. The client saying that he "messed up" has a negative connotation, when the reality is that he is working toward a goal, which often involves setbacks. The client acknowledging that he cannot change what he did is a helpful technique, but it does not change his mindset for the rest of the day. Yoga or other calming activities also do not address all-or-nothing thinking when done in isolation (without a mental reframe); instead, these activities can be used as a diversion to avoid confronting the cognitive distortion completely.

11. C: The best definition of mindfulness includes meditation that involves being aware of thoughts and feelings with no judgment or interpretation and that involves grounding techniques. The goal of mindfulness is to be completely present in your body and to be aware of thoughts and feelings but not to engage in them. Interpretation or radical acceptance of thoughts and feelings would likely escalate thoughts and feelings because they were already distressing for the client. Just controlling cognitions or just controlling the body's response to a situation does not completely support the definition of mindfulness.

12. B: Melatonin is a natural dietary supplement with proven efficacy in improving sleep onset, although it is not recommended as the primary treatment of insomnia. It is available in low doses over the counter and in higher prescription-level doses, and it has no proven negative influences on sleep. Alcohol, although it may help people fall asleep, often affects sleep maintenance because it is disruptive to the sleep cycle. Exercise, if done regularly, can help sleep, but if it is done within 3–4 hours before sleep, it can have a negative impact on sleep quality. The chemicals released during exercise increase the heart rate and body temperature, which can delay the onset of sleep. Drinking a large amount of water near bedtime can disrupt sleep by the need to urinate waking the individual in order to use the bathroom.

13. D: The counselor should always support the diversity of their clients' beliefs despite their own value system. It can be helpful to remember that although the resident may not agree with the client's interpretation of his actions, there is no harm to the client in his goal to refrain from masturbation. Client-centered therapy aligns counseling goals with the client's goals, which in this case involve removing the urges for and eventually the act of masturbation in his life. With this client, it likely would not be helpful to encourage or impose other viewpoints because they would oppose his religious beliefs, and this may also make the client feel unsupported.

Case Study 11

1. A: The MMPI-3 assesses for characteristics of many personality disorders including dependent personality disorder and can provide a large amount of information regarding an individual's personality. Rorschach inkblots can be used in diagnosing dependent personality disorder; however, these tests have low reliability and validity. The SCL-90-R assesses 90 items that include (but are not limited to) depression, anxiety, poor appetite, and hostility. A Likert scale is not an assessment itself; rather, it is a way to scale a response to a question using answer options such as very likely, likely, unlikely, and very unlikely.

2. B: Histrionic personality disorder may appear similar in presentation to dependent personality disorder because the individual with histrionic personality disorder would be seeking assurance and validation from others and may demonstrate the same clingy behaviors. The difference is that a client with dependent personality disorder is less likely to actively engage in behavior for attention and is rather more submissive. Schizoid personality disorder involves a lack of desire to have relationships, and individuals with this disorder are often loners. OCPD is characterized by perfectionism and rigidity with certain tasks and thoughts. Antisocial personality disorder involves behavior that goes against social norms such as deceit and breaking laws.

3. B: This client will need you to establish very clear boundaries because she is likely to become somewhat dependent on you and your sessions with her. With other clients, small amounts of self-disclosure or answering emails outside of sessions may have benefits, but with this client, you may need to insert more explicit guidelines for them. Fees should be appropriate and negotiable as needed. Release of the client's records is up to the counselor's discretion if it might cause harm; otherwise, it is the client's right to have access to her chart. If an assessment is provided, the client should be supported in interpreting the results.

4. C: When processing any sort of trauma, the counselor should follow the client's lead regarding their readiness to discuss the trauma (in this case, abuse). There is no obligation for clients to talk about something that they do not want to, or are not ready to, talk about. It would be helpful to check in every few sessions to show this client that you remember that this was an issue she presented and to open up the opportunity to discuss it, should her willingness/readiness to do so change. Asking about the trauma every session or pressuring the client to talk about the trauma could cause more harm than good and could induce more resistance to openly discuss it. Although it is important to talk about the client's history of physical abuse at some point (because it likely contributes to her presenting issues), the timing must be dictated by the client.

5. A: The psychodynamic approach involves investigating childhood experiences and underlying wishes and fears because they often affect an adult's personality and functioning. Focusing on the present and accepting thoughts and feelings are principles of acceptance and commitment therapy. Changing the narrative from "I'm a loser" to "my anxiety sometimes makes me think I'm a loser" is a principle of narrative therapy, which strives to externalize anxiety as not being part of the client. The use of free association and dream interpretation as well as investigating conscious and unconscious thoughts are parts of psychoanalysis.

6. D: The client signed an informed consent at the start of services, and in doing so she has already agreed that you can report abuse or neglect. Additionally, even if she does not want you to report the abuse, as a mandatory reporter, you are legally required to do so. The age of the client and their cognitive ability are factors that influence the reporting of abuse because adult abuse and neglect includes elderly and intellectually disabled individuals. Having sufficient information also influences the reporting of abuse, because certain elements are necessary to include, such as the name of the abuser.

7. D: Victims of abuse should never be supported in taking any responsibility for the abuse, even if there is evidence of explicit provocation. Although the ex-boyfriend was under the influence and may not have fully known what he was doing, he is responsible for putting himself in a state in which he is not in full control of his actions. The state of intoxication does not protect an individual from owning legal responsibility for their actions.

8. A: Because this client has no history of nonpayment, it would be the most therapeutic course of action to waive the nonpayment fee and allow the client extra time to pay for the session. Generally speaking, fees for the counseling sessions, for late cancellations, and for nonpayment are beneficial for the counselor and the client. The fees ensure that the counselor is paid, and they develop a level of buy-in and accountability for the client to have regular sessions. A blanket rule to apply the fee every time does not take into consideration special circumstances and can harm the counseling relationship. Waiving the fees for the session and nonpayment would not be a good course of action because you do not know at this point if the client will continue to have issues with payments and the client has already agreed to pay for your services.

9. D: It would be inappropriate to accept the gift because the client's diagnosis of dependent personality disorder makes boundaries more complicated and could possibly allow for manipulation. The ACA Code of Ethics does not specify a dollar amount or a clear point of view about when to accept gifts; rather, it focuses on the motivation of accepting the gift or the client's intent for giving the gift. Cultural considerations for accepting or declining gifts are an important consideration; however, the client's diagnosis takes priority in the consideration of accepting gifts.

10. A: The ABC model is used often in CBT and demonstrates the different areas of distress in thought processes. *A* stands for antecedent or an event that occurred, *B* stands for the client's beliefs about the situation, and *C* stands for the consequences of the beliefs. The client's beliefs about the antecedent (buying lunch for herself in the past and being punished for not thinking to do so for her boyfriend) stem from past relationships and lead to her generally being more anxious, feeling as if she has to continue this pattern, and a reduction in anxiety in the moment by doing so but increased anxiety over time. Although her new boyfriend might be happier in the relationship because of these tokens of thoughtfulness, his happiness is not a consequence of her internal belief, which is the focus of the ABC model.

11. C: Paradox is a counseling technique in which the counselor goes along with the client's statement even if they do not agree with it to demonstrate a deeper empathy for the client's underlying feelings. It must be used with care in the counseling relationship. The purpose of using paradox is to investigate the roots of the client's motivation to continue a negative behavior. For instance, this client is frustrated that counseling is taking time and rather than focusing on the client's statement of continuing negative behavior, you are empathizing with this feeling of frustration by agreeing with her statement as an expression of frustration. This statement can also support the client in identifying reasons to change her behavior. The client has the right to start or stop therapy if she wants, but you would want to support her in finding the motivation to participate. Encouraging the client to try new behavior that may have more positive results is a helpful technique, but it does not demonstrate the use of paradox.

12. D: The behavioral experiment that addresses the client's root concern is to buy herself lunch and see if her boyfriend gets offended if she does not buy him lunch, too. He likely will not get offended if she is buying herself lunch when he is not around, and this will provide evidence for the client to use in the future to challenge these intrusive thoughts. It is important for the client to see that she can manage her own anxiety because this builds confidence, but this does not directly confront the source of the anxiety, which is related to offending her boyfriend. The client could simply ask her boyfriend if it would offend him if she did not buy him lunch, but hearing something and experiencing something are different, and she may not believe him based on her past experiences.

13. A: Sigmund Freud's psychoanalytic theory states that there are three parts of the individual's personality: the id, ego, and superego. The id focuses on basic impulses such as aggression and sex. Morals and ideals are part of the superego, and the balance between the two is the ego. The client's own beliefs about functioning are not a part of Freud's view of the human personality.

Tell Us Your Story

We at Mometrix would like to extend our heartfelt thanks to you for letting us be a part of your journey. It is an honor to serve people from all walks of life, people like you, who are committed to building the best future they can for themselves.

We know that each person's situation is unique. But we also know that, whether you are a young student or a mother of four, you care about working to make your own life and the lives of those around you better.

That's why we want to hear your story.

We want to know why you're taking this test. We want to know about the trials you've gone through to get here. And we want to know about the successes you've experienced after taking and passing your test.

In addition to your story, which can be an inspiration both to us and to others, we value your feedback. We want to know both what you loved about our book and what you think we can improve on.

The team at Mometrix would be absolutely thrilled to hear from you! So please, send us an email at tellusyourstory@mometrix.com or visit us at mometrix.com/tellusyourstory.php and let's stay in touch.